B BASS
Bass, Lance,
Out of sync / Lance Bass ;
introduction by Marc Eliot.

OUT OF SYNC

OUT OF SYNC

LANCE BASS

Introduction by Marc Eliot

SSE

SIMON SPOTLIGHT ENTERTAINMENT
New York London Toronto Sydney

SSE

SIMON SPOTLIGHT ENTERTAINMENT

An imprint of Simon & Schuster

1230 Avenue of the Americas, New York, New York 10020

Copyright © 2007 by Lance Bass

All rights reserved, including the right of reproduction in whole or in part in any form.

SIMON SPOTLIGHT ENTERTAINMENT and related logo are trademarks of Simon & Schuster, Inc.

Designed by Gabe Levine

Manufactured in the United States of America

First Edition 10 9 8 7 6 5 4 3 2 1

Library of Congress Cataloging-in-Publication Data

Bass, Lance, 1979–

Out of sync / Lance Bass ; introduction by Marc Eliot. — 1st ed.

p. cm.

ISBN-13: 978-1-4169-4788-2

ISBN-10: 1-4169-4788-4

1. Bass, Lance, 1979– 2. Rock musicians—United States—Biography.

3. 'N Sync (Musical group) I. Title.

ML420.B1863A3 2007

782.42164092—dc22

[B]

2007027132

To my family, friends, and fans

Introduction

The American South has always produced great rock-'n'-roll music and the performers who deliver it to us. Like fiery preachers they bring their message to fervent audiences who seem to live on every word and note. Ever since Elvis, one of the South's favorite sons, youth has had a pop-tune musical signature all its own.

Lance Bass, a member of *NSYNC, the predominant band to come out of Orlando, Florida (via Germany and then all of Europe, echoing the circuitous road the Beatles took to rock-'n'-roll glory), became part of that sound when, as part of *NSYNC, he occupied the hearts and minds of young people everywhere. Likable, good-looking, soft-spoken, and charmingly Southern in his hospitable demeanor, Lance became one of the primal bedroom poster boys for the I-dream-of-you-tonight teenagers of the mid-1990s and early 2000s.

As highly polished as Lance's image was—and it was bright enough to help *NSYNC move more than a million units of its 2001 album *No Strings Attached* the first *day* of its release and two and a half million by that week's end, placing it among a rare handful of albums certified Diamond (sales above ten million units) by the Recording Industry Association of America—it also helped define a generation's sense of liberation, in more ways than one. During a time of relative peace and national prosperity, *NSYNC represented all that was good and clean and healthy in America for its avid young followers all over the world. And yet underneath all that celebration of teenage perfection, for Lance there lurked what to him was a deep, dark, forbidden secret: Lance Bass, all-American teenage boy-band idol, the fantasy-prince hero of girls of all ages, was gay. And because of his place in the band, his upbringing, and the times in which he lived, he felt compelled to plant his flag firmly in the closet of his own fame.

In some circles that might not be a big deal; in Lance's world it meant having everything if you kept your homo-

courage of his own convictions and let the world in on who he really was.

His true journey, then, was not one from obscurity to success, although that certainly defined his playing field. No, the real trip was inner, one of spiritual reconciliation, self-recognition, and self-acceptance. While the rest of the world thought he was the embodiment of unlimited perfection, Lance looked for a reality he could live with. It was a journey that took him around the world and into the stratosphere of pop culture and also brought him to the brink of outer space, even as his own desires took him much deeper into his own soul. It was only when he was pushed to the limit by the prying tabloid press that he was able to discover for himself the true virtues of honesty and openness. The rest of the world may have been surprised at Lance's coming out; to him it became the best party of all. What follows is the remarkable story of a most fascinating, often contradictory, ambitious yet insular young man and the life journey he took, first to acknowledge, then to accept, and finally to celebrate who he really was.

I have gotten to know Lance Bass well and understand that although he is still only in his twenties, he is a veteran rather than a victim of his own past. Too much but not enough of his real life has been misplayed in the tabloids.

sexuality hidden, losing everything if you didn't. Here was a young man who had the same dreams as every other American teenager: to become a rich and famous pop star, to have the adulation of every kid in America in the palm of his hand by doing what he loved most, singing in front of tens of thousands of delirious fans every single night. And Lance made that dream come true without any of the usual struggles that most young musicians have to go through. No playing in dingy clubs night after night for tips; no scrounging on street corners or in subway stations hoping to fill an upside-down hat with enough money to buy a decent dinner; no running away from home in rebellion; no chasing record companies begging for a chance to record. Even Elvis had to drive a delivery truck for a little while.

The problem for Lance was that everything but the singing was a sham. Even as he and the band were being exploited by management (did someone say Elvis?), earning next to nothing as *NSYNC sold millions upon millions of records, there was an inner battle going on that was even tougher to fight and so much harder to win. In a business where image was everything, he knew his was a fake, a shield, a costume for correctness. Lance Bass was his own hyped-up beard, until he found the

The pop star from the South who came "this close" to becoming a space traveler on a Russian Soyuz, who was a member of a group that became the premier pop phenomenon of its decade, and who came out sexually at a time when, in our celebrity-obsessed culture, such disclosure all too often proves to be a career killer, bravely chose truth over image, reality over disguise, life over lies. How he did it is the heart and soul of his story. What follows, then, in his own words, are the details that make up his fabulous, synchronous, high-flying, no-strings-attached, celebrity-filled joyride; they provide a view of Lance Bass, by Lance Bass, you haven't seen before and one you won't easily forget.

—Marc Eliot

Chapter One

I've known I was different ever since I was five years old.
For one thing, I had what I guess you could call innocent
crushes on boys.

I knew it was wrong; at least that's what I was taught
by my family, my church, my friends, my whole world.
That was the overwhelming message I kept on getting.
How could I ever admit to what everyone else believed
was such a bad, even biblically evil thing, especially to my
parents and grandparents, who doted so much on me and
made me feel like I was a little prince?

I understood in my heart it wasn't wrong to be
gay, but I also knew instinctively that I had to play the

game in order to live in the world I was born into.

In all honesty it didn't seem much of a problem to me when I was growing up in Mississippi. There were girls around. I even dated a few, but only because that's what everyone else did. I never thought about it, or felt funny doing it. As for dating guys, it never even entered my thinking that such a thing was possible.

At least not in Mississippi.

That's where I was born, in 1979: the heart of the Deep South. My parents liked the name Lance, so that's what they decided to call me. They'd had it picked out for their firstborn son even before they were married. If they had a boy, they'd agreed, he'd be James Lance Bass, after my dad, James Irvin Bass, Jr. My parents considered making me a III. Thank heavens they settled on Lance!

I was raised in the town of Ellisville, about seven minutes outside of Laurel. Despite my early sexual feelings, I had an extremely happy childhood. I loved my parents, Jim and Diane. I loved my sister, Stacy. And I loved singing in the church choir. My dad was a medical technologist in the Ellisville hospital. I more or less grew up in hospitals, which is why to this day things like having blood work done never freak me out.

We were a completely traditional Southern family. I was brought up a strict Baptist, in the steep shadow of the church where, as it happens, I sang for the very first time. As far back as I can remember, I loved to sing. No one in my family was ever in show business, but my mother's beautiful singing voice put me to sleep each night as a little boy. Even when I'd go off with my dad and grandfather on pheasant hunts in Texas, my mom would tape-record a lullaby so I'd be able to fall asleep in my sleeping bag.

My granddaddy's brother, Uncle Julius, lives near Cape Canaveral. When I was nine years old, my daddy and granddaddy took me to visit him, and that's when I saw my first live space launch. I'll never forget the sight of it! We were there with thousands of people, right near the gigantic countdown clock, the shuttle in the background. Everyone counted down together as the rumble started and the rockets ignited, and the whole thing started rising, shooting straight up into the sky. It was spectacular to think that there were people in there who were actually going into space! That was the day I decided I wanted to be an astronaut when I grew up.

It was something I talked about all the time. Finally, when I turned ten, my parents sent me away for a week one summer to Space Camp at Cape Canaveral. I was certain from then on that my future was to be involved with space. It was the sky, not the stage, that first captured my creative imagination with such an extraordinary display of wonder, probably because singing just came so naturally to me.

My mom taught sixth-grade math at the elementary school I went to, and she remembers that as a toddler I loved singing in our living room for anybody who came to visit. I used to work for hours making up little shows for my parents and their friends, then get all dressed up in costumes that I put together, sometimes performing with my sister.

When I was ten, Dad was transferred to the town of Clinton, in central Mississippi, so the entire family just picked up and moved everything we had from one house to another. Dad happened to know this family in Clinton that was moving to Ellisville, so we simply traded houses. I have to say, the move was both exciting and traumatic for me; I was happy moving to a new place but sad that I had to say good-bye to all of my friends. I knew I was going to especially miss my best friend and next-door neighbor, Brett. He and I had become close playing in the woods that surrounded Ellisville. To me Clinton was, by comparison, a major metropolis. I was a little scared, and I felt a touch of loneliness, a feeling I wouldn't fully understand, or accept, for years to come. Even back then I didn't know how to reach out with my real inner self. I was much better at holding myself back and pretending that things didn't bother me when they did. That was the way of life I had learned, to hold feelings in for the sake of . . . well, for the sake of what, I'm really not sure.

I started fifth grade in Clinton and made the adjustment to my new school fairly easily. Soon enough I had new pals and was enjoying my new life. In seventh grade, when I was twelve, I met a boy named Darren Dale. He quickly became one of my best friends. We did a lot of things together, like fishing and going to the movies, but one thing we really shared was a love of music. That was crucial to me, because music was the only way I had to truly express my feelings while still being able to keep them contained. Other people's songs became vehicles, free rides, in a way. I was only the messenger, or so I wanted people to believe, dressing up the words and music of someone else to make them sound all pretty and sweet. By making the music acceptable I was able to make myself acceptable as well, and for me that was extremely important. I could expose myself and keep myself hidden at the same time.

Both Darren and I sang in the local church choir, but I think Darren, in his way, took it much more seriously than I did. I used it as something of a disguise; he used it to bare his soul. Because of that, I guess, even though we both had pretty good voices, he was often the one chosen between the two of us to take on solos.

This one time there was a school music program that called for a quartet. Darren already belonged to it, and because I had a naturally deep singing voice, he urged me to try out. I made it and became its official bass singer, the first time I ever formally sang in a group. Our debut song was "Sixteen Candles," a pop tune that had been a big hit for a group called the Crests.

I discovered much to my surprise and delight that I had a really good time doing this kind of loose, undisciplined singing, as opposed to choir music, which I'd always found much more restrictive, if also protective. Now I felt free, wanting and able to move around like I was in one of those old fifties bands. I loved the feel of letting go, even this little bit, of letting the inside me out through the ringing harmonies of the quartet. *This is really cool,* I thought to myself, *the way our voices are able to blend without instruments playing behind them.*

My bass voice surprised a lot of people that night. I

remember that after the show my mom and dad asked me where on earth that sound had come from. I didn't know then and I don't know now. For the moment singing would be my only liberation, that voice the only part of me no one had seen before allowed to take shape.

So I smiled and shrugged my shoulders. For the moment I was thrilled that I could please people in this new way. Now I wanted to sing every opportunity I got, in every school and church program that was open to me.

For the next several years music remained my only source of any kind of real freedom, mostly because it relieved me from the dull reality of ordinary everyday schoolwork. So much so that one day when I was thirteen, in the eighth grade, I remember coming home and saying to my dad, "I hope you won't be mad at me if I don't play baseball this year, but I want to try out for the Showstopper group."

He didn't seem to mind at all.

I was relieved at what I took to be his tacit understanding of my situation, at least as much as he could. I'd never been that interested in sports, I guess because I was always the smallest guy on any team I tried out for. Throughout middle school I was always the second shortest kid in my class. The other kids used to call me Half-Pint. It was only when I sang that I felt ten feet tall and was able to convince all the others of my stature. I could hit a note as well as the star quarterback could throw a football.

I naturally gravitated toward the singing crowd, and by this time all my close friends in Clinton were really good singers. The day my friend Darren suggested I try out for the Mississippi Showstoppers, a group he'd been part of already for a couple of years, was the day I decided I would never play team sports again.

The Showstoppers were privately sponsored by the Mississippi Agriculture and Forestry Museum and each member was paid, get this, a hundred dollars a year! We did tons of shows for that hundred dollars, the first money I ever made in show business. I sang a country song for my audition: "I Want to Be Loved Like That." I was so nervous that I was shaking in my fake country cowboy boots. I guess I was all right, because when I finished, right then and there Boyce Vandevere, the Showstoppers director, offered me a place in the show.

Showstoppers was a trip, literally and figuratively. What was so important was learning how to perform like a professional. Every season we came up with a completely new show, and during summer vacations we'd do it somewhere every other weekend. State fairs, political fund-raisers—it didn't matter to me as long as I got to sing.

Those summer dates marked my first exposure to real celebrity. In Mississippi there weren't any local singers I looked up to, but there were always some older Showstopper alumni who'd come back to visit. A lot of them went off and won state-fair singing competitions, and that made them celebrities to me. I remember thinking back then, *Wow, how cool it must be to have someone look up to you that way.*

The only actual celebrity I met back then happened to not be a singer at all: It was quarterback Troy Aikman. I got his autograph when I was twelve, on a church trip to Dallas, Texas. I met him at a mall, where he was getting his hair cut and twenty other kids were pestering him for his autograph. Never did we realize we might be bothering him. Looking back, I know now that meeting Troy Aikman set the tone for how I would eventually treat my own fans. He was so gracious to everyone. A lot of other guys would have gotten annoyed, but he signed his name for all. These days, whenever I think, *No, I don't want to do this,* I remind myself of Troy and I'll sign every autograph and pose for every picture.

Our vocal coach in the Showstoppers was a fellow by the name of Bob Westbrook. Although Bob lived in Memphis, he would drive down to Jackson to coach us and teach us how to sing the music for our shows. In my second year with Showstoppers, my ninth grade or freshman year in high school, Darren and I picked five guys from Showstoppers and formed our own group, Seven Card Stud, to compete in some more state fairs. We did a lot of old fifties stuff—medleys of songs like "Sh-Boom" and "Blue Moon." The three mid-level competitions we won took us to the Mid-South Fair, the state level, in Memphis, Tennessee. I guess you could say it was our regional version of *American Idol.*

We had such starlight in our eyes, we believed we were going to blow everybody away. Then the final votes came back and it turned out we'd lost—*to a girl who was deaf!* The song she sang was "Why Haven't I Heard from You" by Reba McEntire.

Yikes!

Despite that setback, we continued to compete, certain we'd eventually get our ticket to stardom punched. We only got as far as fourth place. However, it wasn't a total loss. Traveling for competitions, I discovered for the first time that there was another world outside of

Clinton, places I could really excel, and not just as a singer. I made a mental note that as soon as I could, I would travel anywhere else where the promise of true freedom seemed to await me.

Seven Card Stud performed in Washington, D.C., and New York City, tailoring each show to fit the location. We did shows for Senator Trent Lott at various social and political affairs. It was great fun and I made a whole lot of new friends.

I also got my first exposure to the phenomenon of screaming girls.

I didn't react the same way as the other guys. I didn't find it titillating or any kind of a turn on, but I loved the energy that was behind it. Again, I had to suppress what I was really feeling in order to be "one of the guys." It wasn't all that hard; it just wasn't me.

When Seven Card Stud played itself out, I thought that that was it: The fun and games were over, and so was my so-called big-time show-business career.

It turned out not to be so. My self-confidence as a singer had grown considerably, along with my desire to expand the boundaries of my world. When the next opportunity came along to break out of the pack, I leaped at it. In my freshman year I tried out for the big high-school show choir we called Attaché. Attaché was, without question, the school's highest singing and social level to achieve, and it provided a chance to appear in its big show each fall and spring. It was like being on *The Corny Collins Show* in *Hairspray*. Getting into Attaché wasn't easy, but I had a good teacher. I just kept following Darren, trying to learn from him, doing what he did, and singing the best I could.

At the end of the year the school posted a list in the hallway of who had gotten in for the following year. I remember seeing Darren's name first, then my own, hardly able to believe it! I was so excited! Only a few slots opened up each year, and I had been chosen. Once again fortune smiled on me and punched my ticket. I was searching, yearning, trying to stretch the limited boundaries of Mississippi for myself, and I had succeeded in doing just that. My voice was my ticket to freedom.

The fall show was usually a big performance at the school, with all eighteen boys and eighteen girls in the group participating. People would come from all over the region to see it. The spring concert was even bigger.

We'd get to take it to Florida, Missouri, Indiana, and Ohio to compete with other schools' Attachés in major national competitions. Our shows were really showcases, the material mostly a combination of Broadway songs like "Beauty and the Beast," current Top 40 pop tunes, and a medley from a classic musical like *Guys and Dolls*, all selected to show off our voices. The training and the touring were invaluable lessons in what today I guess I'd call amateur professionalism. A lot of what I did and learned in Attaché carried over to my work in *NSYNC.

Our director at Attaché was a fellow by the name of David Faire. He was mullet-haired and no-nonsense, but man, could he play the piano and teach music. He'd been brought down from Illinois, and his intensity followed him around like an aura. He's the reason I have the musical and performing concentration and discipline I do today. From the first day he arrived, he was constantly challenging me, yelling at me, sometimes embarrassing me in front of the others, more like a drill sergeant than a director, but he proved to be the best of the best. He could hear a voice go out of tune if he was having a conversation with someone twenty feet away.

David and his wife, Mary, were kind of like a hip-
pie couple. She had long, straight, bright-blond hair with
curly ringlets on the ends, never wore makeup, and made
every costume and every prop we used in Attaché. They
particularly liked seventies rock, especially the group
Journey, so we did a lot of those songs, while wearing silly
sequined costumes that Mary made. It's a wonder I didn't
get my butt kicked wearing something so *fab-u-lous*. But
I didn't care.

Although I always felt very mature for my age, and
most of the adults I came into contact with seemed more
like friends than authority figures, in an oddly likable way
the Faires became surrogate parents, especially when we
were on the road. They watched over us and treated us
like we were their kids. That built a lot of trust in me.
This was something that was to happen over and over
again in my life, sometimes with wonderful results, other
times not so great.

Throughout my time in Attaché, I always had this
feeling that one day I was going to be famous. I just knew
it. At the end of the school year I wrote in my classmate
Keri Martin's yearbook, "Keep this autograph because I'm
going to be famous one day." Even though she was the
one everybody believed was going to be a big Hollywood

star, I just had this gut feeling that something would happen to me, even beyond Attaché, that was going to be very, very special indeed.

In Mississippi you can apply for a driver's license at a younger age than in most other states. I took my first drink when I turned fifteen and got my driver's license later that same year. Once I had it, when I wasn't working with Attaché there was nothing I'd rather do than drive around with my friends.

And date girls.

Even though it wasn't something I wanted to do, I knew that I had to be seen with them, to protect myself, to keep myself in check. Although it might seem to be, it wasn't confusing to me at all. I was very clear on my feelings, and they were separate from what I believed I was supposed to do. Most of all I wanted to fit in, to be one of the guys with all the girls. So I dated, had fun, and proved extremely popular because I never tried to do anything that was considered too forward or out of bounds. I was a very polite, safe date. I guess what saved me most in those days was that I didn't know what true love was. Instead I just imitated what I thought everybody wanted from me, and that got me through the night, so to speak. I played the role of the pleaser and did it very well. Nobody ever suspected a thing inside of me was different from any other Mississippi teenager of the day.

On weekends we'd pile into someone's car, and whoever was driving might pull into the local supermarket, where we'd pick up a six-pack and then hang in the parking lot, everyone's favorite spot, sitting in the car drinking beer and trying to figure out what we wanted to do next.

We'd drive around back roads—we called it "country road ridin'"—while playing silly games, like if a certain song came on the radio, everyone would have to drink a beer, things like that. Someone would always be the designated driver and take us to the middle of nowhere. We'd sit in a circle and sing a song, and whenever anyone messed up, we'd all have to take a drink. We'd hang out for a couple of hours just drinkin', singin', and havin' a good ol' time. Church on Sunday, church on Wednesday, and country road ridin' on Friday night—that was my high life in Clinton, Mississippi.

There were also some favorite local spots we would hit, like the fire tower, or what we called "the other end of 80," which was a little road behind Highway 80 that wrapped around into a dead end. This was where all the local kids really bonded. We'd light a big fire and sit around it for hours, just talking about all that was important in our lives. Again, I played along, giving the others what they wanted, though never daring to go near the darker feelings within, which I couldn't yet quite make out.

We also liked to have parties in our homes where we could all get together and dance and have a little fun with about a dozen of our best high-school friends. No one paired off romantically, which was a great relief to me. We all just sort of hung out together.

One thing I loved to do back then and still do today is throw parties—especially at Halloween. One Halloween I hosted a *Clue*-themed party. That was my favorite movie at the time. All my friends got dressed like the characters. We made a home video of it and whenever we'd watch it we'd laugh our heads off. That was my directorial debut.

I remember one Halloween night more than any of the others. We were hanging out at the supermarket parking lot. As usual there was nothing special to do, so we decided to go halfway across town to our friend Nathan's house, about a seven-minute drive from where we were. I was in my friend Jason's car, a little white two-door job with a muffler that dragged along back on the ground. It was almost impossible to get in and out of that car if you were sitting in the back; I got in and it was so cramped that I could barely even put on my seat belt. Just as we were about to pull out, one of my friends, Laura, came over, tapped on my window, and asked me to ride with her. I told her no way, I was already buckled into this sardine can and I wasn't about to get out. But she was adamant and wouldn't let up. Finally I squeezed myself out and rode with her.

When we got to Nathan's house, we waited for forty-five minutes and there was no sign of him. As it turned out, the car Jason was driving and Nathan was riding in had been involved in a terrible wreck. The car spun around and hit another car, and the back end, where I'd been sitting only minutes earlier, was totaled. It looked like an accordion. If Laura hadn't forced me out of Nathan's car, I could have been seriously injured.

On Halloween!

While I have vivid, fun memories of those times, I remember hardly anything about my school classes. When I look back now, I realize how unprepared for the real world I actually was. Forget about regular lessons—nothing interested me except singing! Lucky for me I was able to put that to good use; otherwise who knows where I would have wound up. I guess I just seemed to know that something special was going to happen to me.

In fall 1995, my junior year, I was elected vice president of our class and was put in charge of the float for the homecoming parade—a very big deal. Every grade had to make a float to compete with the others, and it became very intense. There'd be float parties, and of course the sophomores would get egged and we'd destroy their floats—all the good stuff! Our football team was going to play the Hornets, a team from a nearby school, so I came up with the idea to make a giant Raid can. To make the "spray," we borrowed David Faire's smoke machine that he used for his shows, and with that we'd "raid the Hornets." It was all great fun. By the way, we tied the seniors, even though our float was so much better. Of course!

Friday afternoon was the big homecoming parade, which was awesome, and then on Saturday night I would be going to the homecoming dance with my friend Lacey. She was a year older than me, which felt normal because I always hung out with older kids. It also meant she knew a lot more—how to drink, how to smoke, all the "cool" stuff.

It wasn't until I got home from the parade that I

found out my mother had received a call from a woman by the name of Lynn Harless. Her son, Justin Timberlake, wanted to know if I'd be interested in joining a new pop group called *NSYNC.

I was in the kitchen when Mom came in and asked me if I knew who Justin Timberlake was.

I had heard of him; he was one of the kids on *The Mickey Mouse Club*. Then she told me about the phone call.

All I could do was stare back at her in disbelief.

Chapter Two

Orlando was the place to be in the nineties. There was a musical identity there as strong as any in the history of pop. I guess it started with the updated *Mickey Mouse Club*, which produced such future stars as Britney Spears, Christina Aguilera, Keri Russell, Ryan Gosling and yes, Justin Timberlake. When Disney revived the *Mickey Mouse Club* TV show, it was only a matter of time before a new generation of pop stars would emerge. *The Mickey Mouse Club* was a sort of junior-league MTV, maybe a little more squeaky clean and innocent, but no less popular than anything else that young people, including me, watched every day.

So you can imagine my surprise when I came home that day and found out that the mother of a guy who was on *The Mickey Mouse Club* had called, inviting me to try out for this new group. I felt excited and lucky. I know a lot of would-be musicians spend years struggling to make it. They play small clubs; they live day to day, hand to mouth, playing for maybe a dozen people a night. I had done none of that. Every time I'd left home with any of the groups I sang with, we always had enthusiastic, packed houses.

The way Justin and his mom came to me was an interesting bit of luck on my part. Bob Westbrook, my vocal coach while I was with the Mississippi Showstoppers, is from Memphis, Justin's hometown. He coached a very young, pre-Mouseketeer Justin.

Bob thought of me when Lynn and Justin said they were looking for a bass singer for this new band. They already had the first four guys chosen.

Bob told them he knew this kid in Mississippi who could really sing, but that they might have a problem getting me to Florida because I was only sixteen and would need my mother's consent, and Bob knew my mother was very skeptical about show business. He was sure she wouldn't let her son just run off and join a band. That's when Lynn decided to call my mother directly and see if she could maybe change her mind.

Lynn talked to my mother for a long time and explained to her how they wanted me to join this new pop group based in Florida, how she knew there was nothing to worry about because her own son was in it, and that it had the same kind of quality and supervision as everything Disney produced in Orlando involving young people. When she was finished, my mom said, politely but firmly, "I don't think so," thanked her, and hung up.

The phone rang again a few minutes later. This time it was Bob Westbrook. Obviously, Lynn had called him for support. "Mrs. Bass," he said, "I'm not telling you what to do, but I know Lynn, and any project she would allow her son to be involved in is going to be on the total up-and-up. I know the family and they're good people. You should at least give her the benefit of the doubt and check it out. It might be a very good thing for Lance."

And there was still another call after that. This one was from Lou Pearlman, founder of Trans Continental Records, Inc. He also tried to convince my mom to just bring me down to Orlando for a tryout, and if he liked what he saw, they could discuss what to do from there. "What's the harm in that?" he asked. He promised to fly my parents and me down for a weekend, all expenses paid. Mom said she would think it over. I thought at this point she might be softening her stance ever so slightly and would at least consider the possibility of letting me audition for the group.

The afternoon went by and the calls kept coming. The next one was Lynn again, and this time she put Justin on an extension line to talk directly to my mom. Somehow together they managed to convince my mom to bring me to Orlando, if only to see what all the fuss was about.

I was beside myself with excitement. I wanted to go so badly, I never even guessed that my mom had had a problem with any of it. Because I was underage I was going to need my parents' consent, but I knew that no matter what my mom decided, there was no way I wasn't going to Orlando. The more we talked it over, the more my mom began to realize it was hopeless to try to stop me. When she finally said I could go, I was so excited I could hardly stand still!

I was so pumped I wanted to leave right then, but I was supposed to go to the homecoming dance the following night. I attended it, but I couldn't concentrate on anything else—so much so that I didn't even go to the hotel after party, where the *real* fun of homecoming always takes place. I wanted to go home early because a flight to Orlando had been booked for us early Sunday morning by Justin's mother and Lou Pearlman, the manager of the group. The idea was for me to meet the other boys and for them to meet me, to test out the waters to see if there was any real chemistry between us. I really didn't know what to expect, except that from the moment the first phone call had come in, I'd had no doubt that I would be in the group and that we would all be enormously successful. I wasn't letting my ego lead me around or anything; that's just the way I felt, deep inside. Pretending that something has already happened keeps me focused and self-assured. I guess it's a form of faith. Being so young, I had very little experience to call on, but I had loads of faith.

We arrived on a warm, sunny day, like every other day in Orlando. Lynn and Lou were waiting for us at the airport. Lou had personally driven with Lynn in his Rolls-Royce, and that was the chariot he used to take us all to the Enclave, this really great hotel where he had booked rooms for us. After we unpacked, we were driven to a big house where the other guys in the band were living.

The first thing I saw was Chris Kirkpatrick playing hockey with Justin in the driveway. We all got out of the car, and while my mom and dad talked with Lynn and

Lou, I went over to meet them. I was feeling very shy. Everything was happening so fast, and now for the first time I felt a little self-conscious, knowing that I was completely out of my familiar Mississippi surroundings.

I introduced myself and was able to get out all of maybe two words without stumbling over myself as I tried to make polite conversation. The others were friendly, but at this point I'm sure they didn't know quite what to make of me. Chris was the more outgoing of the two, and I sensed he was trying to make me feel relaxed and comfortable. He told me he was from Pittsburgh and had gone to college with Howie Dorough from the Backstreet Boys, which was how he had first encountered Lou Pearlman and pitched him the idea of starting *NSYNC.

Justin, on the other hand, played it cool. I could tell immediately he was to be the official "cool cat" of the group, even if he was all of fourteen years old. That didn't seem to matter. He was obviously focused and already a very "seasoned" entertainer, having started his professional singing career at the age of three. A few minutes later they took me inside to meet JC Chasez, another *Mickey Mouse Club* alumnus.

JC struck me as kind of being in his own world, a guy

who did his own thing, and also the mature one in the group. He wasn't the oldest—Chris was—but he acted that way. I could tell he had been around and seen a lot.

Joey Fatone was really nice, friendly, open, very talkative, and very foul-mouthed. When he was thirteen his family had moved to Orlando, like a lot of New York families do when they want to get away from the cold. He went to high school in Orlando, which is where he met Chris and JC. Joey is that charismatic type of chorus kid everyone knows in high school. He was always singing the lead and effortlessly the most popular guy around.

It occurred to me at this point that since no one had even heard me sing a lick yet, it might be a good idea not to get too friendly with anyone, because this might well turn out to be a very brief visit. I didn't know it at the time, but they had already lost another guy who'd joined the group as its bass singer. Unfortunately, he'd only lasted three days before leaving, apparently not wanting to do the teen music thing. That was maybe the worst career choice he'll ever make. For at least some period soon thereafter, he worked at a pizza parlor. As it turned out, though, his decision to leave would be the best one in the world for me.

And this was something I really wanted. For one thing, I liked the fact that it was an all-boy group. I felt comfortable around these guys and believed I wouldn't have to play the "girl" game with anybody in the group. For another, I sensed this could be my ticket out of Mississippi. It wasn't that I didn't like home. My parents were the best, my sister was great, I loved where I lived, and school had given me a chance to sing. It was just that I felt there was a big world out there, and somewhere in it was a place for me. I was hoping this was going to be the way for me to start the major journey of my life, the one that would lead me—the real me—to myself.

A little later that same day Lou called all of us back inside to meet Robin Wiley, a young woman who was going to work with the band. She had been the vocal coach for *The Mickey Mouse Club*, which is how Justin and JC knew her. She was also one of Lynn Harless's best friends. Robin was also a supertalented singer-songwriter who, from day one, wrote much of our material, arranged all our harmonies, and gave the band what would come to be known as its signature sound.

Now she took us to another room, where we started singing together. This, I knew, was going to be my biggest test. I ran up and down some scales, did a little singing, and performed the one full song I had prepared, "Old Man River." I'd chosen it because it was a classic show tune that was built around a bass voice as the lead.

When I finished, she said she wanted to hear what I sounded like with the guys. She showed me the bass part for her arrangement of "The Star-Spangled Banner." Although I'd sung the anthem hundreds of times in school, I'd never done it in harmony before—that is, singing a part completely different from what everyone else was singing. We tried it together a cappella, meaning without instruments, and as our voices blended together I got chill bumps all over. When we finished, a hush came over the entire room. Everybody had heard what I had and could feel the moment. It was like, *Wow, what a sound!* The way the harmonies came out was like nothing I'd ever heard before.

Robin smiled and was the first to speak. "I think we found our bass." And the boys agreed!

My mother was able to hear all that went on through the closed door and knew right then and there that I was not going back to Mississippi with her to live. She was right. As of October 1, 1995, I became the newest member of a new Orlando-based band called *NSYNC.

*   *   *

I knew that I had to start taking care of myself and not rely on anyone else. My talent had gotten me this far; now I had to make sure I stayed where I wanted to be. Almost immediately I started prepping for our debut showcase and getting comfortable settling into the house. Dad took the contract Lou Pearlman had drawn up to a lawyer he knew in Mississippi, who went through it and said it was fine, a standard show-business agreement that was okay for them and me to sign. There was a set time from Lou to get it returned to him, so Dad brought it to Mom at the school where she taught for her signature. She still remembers crying as she signed it. She was only hoping they were doing the right thing and was terrified that they weren't.

While I was in Orlando, my mom gathered my lessons from school for the next two weeks. I was preparing for our showcase: learning dance steps and new music, and sitting for wardrobe fittings. I worked with Robin every day on my singing. I started learning with the other guys the songs that Lou had specifically chosen for us to perform and eventually record.

And I loved every minute of it. I felt oddly freed from

the shackles of my small-town life. Don't get me wrong, I loved Mississippi and all my friends, but here there were no expectations about me except that I could sing and dance. I didn't have to pretend I was something I wasn't. I just had to hope I was something they thought I was. The other guys and I were in this together, as one. We were all going to grow up together.

It was an exhausting schedule, but it didn't matter to me because I remained totally pumped throughout our rehearsals. My parents, meanwhile, were, at least externally, completely supportive. They knew how badly I wanted this and that I would have made their lives miserable if they hadn't let me pursue the opportunity.

We did our first live showcase exactly nineteen days after I first arrived, on October 20, 1995: four songs completely harmonized and choreographed. I have to say I was the worst dancer in the world (Joey always describes my dancing as very "white," meaning, well, good enough to get by but not great) when I began to learn the steps they had worked out for us, and everyone in the band knew it. I had only done some show-choir dancing before, which was nothing as precise as this. It was hard for me at first, and I wasn't sure I was ever going to be able to get the hang of it. Chris couldn't dance very well either. As the time for the showcase neared, we both learned how to fake it really well.

The showcase was videotaped at Pleasure Island before an audience of about a hundred *Mickey Mouse Club* fans, with parts of it intended for our demo video Lou needed to pitch to record companies. At the time we thought we were so great—after all, we'd only been together nearly two weeks—but, looking back, it was so *horrible*, I don't see how we ever got a deal from it. I would have to laugh out of pity if someone tried to sell me *NSYNC today based on that demo.

Nevertheless, by the time we took the stage I felt ready. We were all in new, matching costumes and hair-dos. Being a Mississippi boy, I'd always had my hair long on the top, sheared on the sides, and the way it looked in the morning was essentially the "style." Out of despera-tion, I think, Lou hired this girl to come in and redo my hair. She cut it evenly and dyed it orange—it was sup-posed to be blond but didn't quite turn out that way—with an awful greasy comb-over. I didn't like it but went along because that's what Lou and the others said they wanted. I wound up wearing my hair that way for the next year and a half. Ew.

Just before we went onstage together for the first time, I looked at myself in a full-length mirror and thought, *Who is that guy and what is he doing?* Like my hair, everything was changing and happening so fast that I didn't have time to think about any single part of it too much. Or what was going on inside of me, although I knew that that was at least as exciting. I was shedding my old, protective (or was it restrictive?) skin. I was doing more than re-emerging; I was being reborn.

From this show on and for the next seven years, the pace would never slacken. The others seemed already like hardened professionals, looking to amplify who they already were. But I wasn't the only one having a bit of an anxiety attack before the first show. Chris was on the backstage fire escape throwing up. If I'd had a second longer to think about it, I might very well have turned tail, taken off, and run as fast as I could. After all, new beginnings aren't always so easy. Thankfully, however, none of us had any more time to think about it before we took the stage and put on our show.

Suddenly I was out there in front of these hundred kids, singing our four prepared songs—a cover of the Beatles' "We Can Work It Out"; one Lou Pearlman claimed to have written, called "I Want You Back for More" (we eventually found out it had been recorded by another group—same tune, different lyrics—a little while earlier); and two others I believe were written by JC. Somehow, we got through it in one piece! I can still remember the surge of good feelings I got when it was over, as I left the stage to the enthusiastic applause of all those kids. I loved the sound of that, that they were applauding the me that I knew I was.

I wanted more.

And then it was over, at least for the moment. With our showcase in the can, there was nothing left to do but wait for Lou to make a deal for the band. I had no choice but to return to school the following Monday.

During physics I told my teacher all about the show, and she got so excited that she insisted we stop everything so the whole class could watch the demo tape together. That's the moment I knew something very basic had changed in my life. All the other kids were watching, in awe and with tremendous excitement, something I had already done. My geographical locus and my cultural priorities had irrevocably shifted from Clinton, Mississippi, to Orlando, Florida. And that was only the first step on my way to the whole world.

* * *

Meanwhile, back in Orlando, Lou Pearlman was send-
ing out that demo to all the record companies, looking
to get a distribution deal. At the same time, completely
sure he was going to get us signed, he began planning a
big tour for *NSYNC. In January I returned to Orlando
to prepare for it, and both Justin and I enrolled in a
special University of Nebraska program that specialized
in homeschooling. I was assigned two teachers, who
helped me finish the last of my high-school requirements in four months, and years later, when I did the
celebrity *Who Wants to Be a Millionaire* TV show, they
were my experts. Part of me had wanted to graduate
high school with my class, with all my old friends whom
I'd lately been missing a lot, but the other part wanted
to go on the road with *NSYNC as a professional musi-
cian. I was torn between the two, but the stronger pull
was definitely *NSYNC.

We were busy every minute of the day. If I wasn't
studying, I was in the studio with the other guys working
on songs. The coolest thing about that for me was recording tracks at Shaquille O'Neal's place. He had a complete
professional recording studio called Twism built right
into his house.

I couldn't believe I was actually singing in Shaq's house. He was away with the team, so of course I checked out the place. The thing that struck me most was how big everything was. He had this dining room table that was large enough to seat, well, a basketball team. I'd never seen home furniture that size before. One day when I wasn't there, Shaq actually showed up in person and met Justin and Chris. I was so jealous!

Most of our time was spent in an old warehouse, where we rehearsed the dance parts of our stage show. It was always a hundred and twenty degrees with no air-conditioning. I was drenched in sweat as I learned all kinds of interesting skills, like how to dance and sing while holding a microphone. I was never all that good at learning the choreography and because of it had to work twice as hard as the others just to keep up. But I could sing a great bass part, and that kept me on good footing with everyone.

I was having a blast and my parents knew it. To try to keep an eye on me, to protect me—remember, I was only sixteen years old—my dad transferred to a hospital in Orlando, while Mom stayed in Clinton where my sister, Stacy, was in school. They also sold the family home so they could keep an apartment in each state. We were all together as much as we could be, with Mom and Stacy coming down on the weekends and in the summer.

Lou personally supervised everything we did. He was in control. It was his idea that pop bands like us could be the next big thing: That belief came to him because at one time he used to lease planes, and one of his lease clients was the pop band New Kids on the Block. He saw what they were doing and the kind of money they were making and felt he could do the same thing and make even more. At the same time he met Johnny Wright, who was New Kids' road manager. Lou and Johnny became friends, and when Lou decided to put a boy band together, he got Johnny to join him; that, in a nutshell, is how the idea for the Backstreet Boys was born. Lou decided to do it all over again with *NSYNC, this time building a band around Chris's vision of a singing group.

I always liked Lou a lot, right from the first time I met him. He was this large man who seemed so happy all the time. He had a way of making you feel special. He loved to lay out the red carpet every time he saw us, and I thought he must have been the wealthiest man who ever lived to be able to do the kinds of things he did and give us the support he insisted we needed. He had all these limos and Rolls-Royces and was always using them to take us to great dinners in upscale restaurants. I trusted him and felt we were in the right hands. I felt I had a genuine friendship with "Papa Lou," as he insisted we all call him, and that it was going to last forever.

Of course it wasn't until much later that we all realized that in fact *we* were paying for everything: the dinners, the clothes, the transportation, all of it was recoupable by Papa Lou, and was to come out of our profits.

But at the time he was easy to talk to, totally supportive, and he had this mantra that he kept repeating to all of us at every opportunity: "You're gonna be big . . . you're gonna be huge, huge . . . *huge*, I tell ya!"

To have that support at so early a stage of our development was awesome, especially because according to Lou, his partners in the parent company, Transcon (Trans Continental Records, Inc.) didn't even know about us. He was keeping us hidden from them, or so he said, because being the small, independent company it was, it already had its hands full trying to break the Backstreet Boys. Everyone there loved them. They had just recorded their first record and were about to go off to Germany, where something called the boy-band phenomenon was peaking. Lou gave us a code name—"B5"—so no one would know he had another boy band that he was trying to get on the same label.

At least that's what he told us at the time. The truth was, everyone at Transcon already knew all about *NSYNC, and as much as everyone there loved the Backstreet Boys, they seemed concerned that we were going to steal their thunder.

Meanwhile, Lou became sort of an unofficial sixth member of *NSYNC. That didn't mean he became a groupie, like a DJ or PR guy who decided it might be fun to live and work with the band. What it meant was that he was entitled to a sixth of everything we earned (on top of what he got for being our manager, our record company, and our publisher). "Don't worry about anything," he'd tell us whenever one of us, or our parents, would inquire as to the state of our finances. "You just do the singing and dancing and I'll take care of the rest." We were so young and innocent, we had no trouble believing him. We even helped him convince our skeptical moms and dads.

That blind trust would later come back to haunt us all.

At this early stage I was far more concerned about getting along and fitting in with the other four members of the band than about how much money I was making. Chris, as I said, was the friendliest and most welcoming toward me. I could tell he wanted to make me feel comfortable, which I greatly appreciated. He was always talking to me and cracking funny little jokes. He was an interesting guy. He had just missed getting into the Backstreet Boys. He was the sixth man chosen, or the first runner-up. He was incredibly disappointed and went to Lou to ask if he would listen to demos from another band. When Lou said yes, Chris went ahead and formed the nucleus of what became *NSYNC. He talked to JC from *The Mickey Mouse Club* and asked him if he'd be interested in joining a new group. JC said he couldn't because he was working with Justin Timberlake on an album of their own. At the time, *The Mickey Mouse Club* had just ended its run, and the two of them were planning to become a duo.

"That's okay," Chris said. "He can be in the group as well."

One night after agreeing to work together, the three went out to a place called Eight Tracks, a seventies-style club at Pleasure Island. On the dance floor was Joey Fatone, who is a really good dancer, as the rest of America has since discovered. Chris, who knew Joey from when they'd both worked at Universal Studios—Chris was part of the Hollywood Hi-Tones, an a cappella group there, and Joey had worked at Beetlejuice's Graveyard Revue—thought he might make a good addition to the group. The next day they tried Joey out on bass, which is where they wanted to use him, but being a baritone singer he didn't quite cut it on bass. They liked Joey and decided to keep him anyway and to keep looking for the bass part, so the group would increase to five members.

Despite our initial burst of enthusiasm and the warm welcome our showcase received, we weren't going anywhere. By August 1996, nearly a year after I'd been flown in to audition for the group, we had not progressed at all. I became so discouraged I lost that sense of liberation I had first experienced. Now I felt lonely for my home in Mississippi and my friends. Rather than continue to work with my tutor, I wanted to finish my senior year in Clinton and graduate with my class, and fly back to Orlando when and if it became necessary. I could tell the others felt the same way, that we were going nowhere, and fast.

Everything changed the very day I made up my mind to go back to Mississippi. Just as I was packing, I got the call from Johnny telling us that BMG Ariola Munich, a

German division of BMG, had offered *NSYNC a deal, to be brokered through Transcon, and that they wanted us to relocate to Germany to make our first album.

That happened because Johnny, who had become impatient with the band's lack of progress, had decided to officially take over the reins as our manager; he'd personally taken our demos around to shop us for a deal. Before that, Lou had more or less played the role of our manager, and in my view, he hadn't done much of a job. Within a month Johnny got three companies interested: RCA, Sony, and BMG Ariola Munich. There was a reason for BMG's sudden interest in us. They already had the biggest band in Europe, Take That, but popular band member Robbie Williams had just dropped out of the group. His departure not only threatened the future of the group but caused general pandemonium across the continent. Young girls especially were crushed by the news and were threatening to jump off roofs all over Europe.

They say that timing is everything, and in our case it proved to be true. We didn't know about any of the Take That stuff. What we did know was that BMG Ariola Munich was distributing the Backstreet Boys' label, Jive Records, but Jive and BMG had clashed over some issues unrelated to Backstreet. Because of that dispute BMG knew they weren't going to get another album out of Backstreet Boys anytime soon, if ever; they needed another act immediately, and that turned out to be us. Johnny convinced some BMG executives to come to our new Pleasure Island showcase, and they signed us on the spot to BMG Ariola Munich.

So I continued to pack my bags—only not for Mississippi. The next day I flew to Munich along with the other guys, Lou Pearlman, Johnny Wright, and Lynn Harless. My parents couldn't go because they were working. For the first time in my life I was about to leave the country. I was ecstatic!

I had been out of the country for about two weeks when I started to feel homesick. I called my mom and told her she would love it here and that she needed to come out. Mom told me she couldn't, that she was still working. "But, Mom," I said, pleading, "I need you." And that was all it took. She could hear her little boy calling for her and did not hesitate to respond. She up and quit her job and had joined our caravan by the next week.

Feeling safe and secure, with Mom by my side, I was ready to face my future. And what a future it would turn out to be!

Chapter Three

No sooner did we land in Munich, check into our hotel, and unpack than we had to *repack* and return to the airport, headed this time for Stockholm, Sweden, where BMG wanted us to record our first song, "I Want You Back."

Because this was my first time in Europe, the first thing I really wanted to do was go to a pub and have a beer. I just wanted to see if I could get away with it. At the earliest opportunity Joey and I went across the street and tried to order a round of Guinness. The waitress asked for my ID because she didn't believe I was eighteen (I wasn't; I had only just turned seventeen). I told her I'd left it back at the hotel; she shrugged and gave me the beer anyway. I thought that was so cool.

After the first sip, though, all my euphoria left me; it was the worst beer I'd had in my life.

But I loved Stockholm. I can remember sitting at McDonald's with Joey and being amazed at how beautiful everybody was. Beautiful blonde after beautiful blonde, like an endless lovely dream. Once we were settled in, we started making regular trips to the Cheiron Studios where Denniz Pop had produced all these great records for ABBA, Backstreet Boys, and Robyn. After a week or so we finished our first two singles: "I Want You Back" and "Tearin' Up My Heart." The first time I heard them on the playback, I couldn't believe how great we sounded. Denniz knew how to make records, and it showed. He was able to maximize every part of our voices until we sounded like a hundred-man choir (to me, anyway). The songs moved and were complex, yet easy to listen to, catchy in that pop-tune way I loved. As it turned out, every major hit we had in our first go-around came out of those Stockholm studios. The record company loved our approach and put a concept behind it intended to define our image the way they saw us. As far as they were concerned, there was no question that we were going to be the Next Big Thing.

Now that Take That had split up, the Backstreet Boys took over as the number one boy band in Europe. By the way, "boy band" was a description that every one of us—in both groups—hated. What did it mean? To me it sounded like a bunch of kids held together by their mother's rubber band so they wouldn't get lost. Worse, dozens of so-called boy bands had sprung up all over the place, each trying to be the Next Big Thing. Most of them had no talent at all and couldn't hide that fact no matter how much production they had. In person most of them were lip-synchers, one-hit wonders or less. To me "boy band" was a demeaning title because it took what we did and how we thought of ourselves—as a real group of performers who could sing in close harmony and move really well—and turned us by definition into something cheesy and assembly-line.

*NSYNC arrived on the European pop scene fast and strong primarily because of the kind of advance work that Lou Pearlman specialized in. It felt like as soon as we finished unpacking, he had us on the cover of every magazine in Germany and the rest of Europe, even before "I Want You Back" was released. It was a crazy and exciting time.

Yes, here I was, just seventeen and living in a foreign country that was, unlike Mississippi, very, very open-minded. It was strange to be somewhere and not know what people were saying when they spoke, not be able to read the headlines in the local papers. But I knew what I felt: I was like a flower that had been kept indoors, nourished by an artificial light, suddenly planted in the middle of this most beautiful sun garden. And I was more than ready to blossom.

We toured around on a double-decker bus and had girls throw themselves at us left and right. It was insane. And very fun. We all lived the rock star life for a while. Girls were all over us, and it was weird for a shy, young, naive kid like me with different sexual feelings to see that. There was a period where I could have had any girl I wanted, if I had wanted any of them. I didn't find the groupie thing particularly interesting or meaningful. Of course, the other guys in the band didn't feel that way, and I can't say I blame them. We all had a lot of respect for each other. If I didn't participate sexually, I was around enough of it for no one to suspect that it wasn't my thing on any level.

The guys are pretty private, and as much partying as went on they were fairly discreet. They all got their share, I'm sure, as much as you can imagine and probably a whole lot more, but they tried to maintain some public image of innocence, in keeping with this goofy idea that we were "boys" in a band. After shows we went out for fun. We met a lot of girls, and a lot of girls found their way back to the hotel (my mom always went to bed early, thank God). We were teenagers and it seemed like the natural thing to do. If I couldn't sleep, and funny enough I could never sleep if I went to bed too early, I could go to the window of my hotel room, wherever we were, and even if it was three o'clock in the morning there would be hundreds of young girls in the parking lot waiting for one of us to take a peek out. As soon as I'd part the curtains, they'd start screaming and taking pictures. It was insane and funny. We never took it too seriously, we never thought it was meaningful, so we played along just for the fun of it.

For me there were many times when I felt I had to go along with the guys so that they wouldn't suspect I might have a different agenda. Between them and my mom's presence, there was very little opportunity for me to explore my own desires. In all the time we were in Europe, I never had a single sexual encounter with a guy. Partly because there wasn't a lot of temptation, since there were never any guys around—my bandmates made sure of that because they didn't want any competition, or worse, angry boyfriends and fathers—and partly because I was simply afraid to risk my standing in the band. Although I will say this—anyone gay in Europe was a lot more easily accepted than he would have been in the States. That was an eye-opener for me, one of the things I noticed that considerably broadened my perspective about life. I loved the easy acceptance, the feel in the air that anything that happened between two people was fine.

All the other guys were more than ready to take advantage of their positions, especially Joey. He's always been a big flirt, and the girls seem to love him that much more for it. Joey loved all the attention, especially from girls who were well-endowed. In many ways he epitomized the modern pop star on tour. He was more of a flirt than anything more serious, though, because he was already dating his high-school sweetheart, Kelly, and would eventually marry her (and, I might add, have a beautiful daughter named Brianna whom I am proud to call my goddaughter).

JC had girlfriends off and on, but he remained the "mature" member of the band, even on the road. He became like our dad. He almost never went out and partied with us after shows, while the rest of us, including me, partied every night. Although we were always all together, traveling on buses, rehearsing, eating, sleeping, I hung mostly with Joey, who was always a little too busy to notice or wonder why I wasn't taking advantage of the girl situation. I would talk to the girls, hang with them, and maybe drink a little, but I managed most of the time to wind up alone in bed.

Looking back, I don't know how we did it. We'd average about four hours of sleep a night. It felt like every second of our offstage time was taken with promotion. We did every radio show in Europe, every TV show, and sat for interviews with every teen magazine and there seemed to be millions of them. And following every performance we'd all go out and party. There was always an after party, and we'd use the opportunity to act like teenagers, because that was what we were. It was our youth that let us stay up all night and still be fresh and sweet in the morning, ready to do it all over again.

That New Year's Eve we flew to Mainz, Germany, where we taped a TV special, after which we all got into cars to go to Cologne, Germany, to do another one. It was unusual to have two TV appearances booked in two different cities. We only had a limited amount of time in between, so we drove a hundred and forty miles an hour on the autobahn to make them both. My mom was with us, and she was completely on edge because of how fast we were going, so fast the car was shaking. To me it was the perfect metaphor for our careers. We were racing along at top speed. Everything we wanted, our slightest wish, was granted as if a genie had been assigned to the band. And we never saw a bill for anything. It was like being kids in the candy store, only the candy was our audience.

A lot of paparazzi and fans were following us, way too close for comfort. In Europe the paparazzi and fan situation is so much bigger than it is in America. In the States no fans ever followed our tour bus or ran after us the way thousands of girls did in Germany. A couple of times they almost ran us off the road. More than once we had to stop so that our bodyguards could warn them that they had to back off or someone was going to get hurt.

It also made me think about how crazy our lifestyle was so quickly becoming. It felt like we were going through something I can only describe as what Beatlemania must have been like back in the sixties, especially since, as the Beatles had, we'd begun our push into the big time in Germany. When "I Want You Back" was released and became a smash, there seemed to be even more girls than ever.

Girls would hide in room-service carts to get into our rooms. Girls would jump on airport luggage conveyer belts to get across security and closer to our planes. We could never wear any kind of jewelry, because it would get ripped right off our bodies. I had never experienced anything like it in my life. It seemed like thousands of young girls were forever chasing us down the street, after us if we were on foot, or following our bus once we somehow managed to get inside it. It was wild and crazy and while I loved the attention, the other guys loved . . . well, the *attention.*

We had hit the ground running and never let up. We followed "I Want You Back" with "Tearin' Up My Heart," and our back-to-back hits helped us push all the other boy bands out of the way as we rose to the top of the charts. When our first album, *NSYNC,* was released in Germany on May 26, 1997, it shot to number one like it had been blown out of a cannon. We were bigger than the Beatles ever were in their German stage. Nobody could touch us now.

For the next year and a half we worked morning, noon, and night: We rehearsed our stage show, we recorded, we did tours, we promoted the album at every radio station in Europe. And when we weren't performing, we were in rehearsing rooms polishing our live act, striving to make it even better than it already was. I had to learn all the new steps and the harmonies, work in the studio, and then on performance days be ready to do a show. It was nonstop high pressure, but I loved it, especially the recording part.

*NSYNC traveled the continent—Switzerland, Austria, the Netherlands, France, Spain, Belgium, Poland, and Germany—always promoting the band. Because of the tightness of our schedules and the constant traveling time between shows, I got to see very little of the actual countries. We passed through Paris half a dozen times and I've actually never seen the Eiffel Tower up close, let alone been inside it.

We were lucky if we got four hours of sleep a night, but we didn't care, because it was all so new, different, and exciting! I think one of the reasons I still suffer from insomnia is because of the crazy sleep patterns we fell into. To this day I'm a night owl. I love to stay up late and wake up late.

Being in *NSYNC made me respect anybody who has ever achieved anything in show business. I'm still such a geek when it comes to entertainers. I just love meeting performers. Every time we performed with a new artist on the bill, I always wanted to meet them, get to know them, and hang out. Also, it was odd for me to see some of my favorite entertainers coming backstage to meet us. At times I couldn't believe I was standing with the likes of Gloria Gaynor, Tom Hanks, the Rolling Stones, Goldie Hawn, and Alice Cooper. We especially loved the Stones and played their music before our shows at every concert. Keith Richards came to many of our shows and always insisted that a bottle of Jack Daniel's be waiting for him at the sound board. I remember one time during our show—the part when we flew out over the stage—looking down and seeing Keith smiling, Jack in one hand, flipping us off with the other!

In a funny way *NSYNC reminded me of high school and my days with Attaché. Here I was, making music and traveling and running into the same young bands over and over again. I'm talking about Destiny's Child, Britney Spears, 98 Degrees, Backstreet Boys, etc. We were MTV-generation artists working the same circuit, just like the Attaché competitions.

While I loved all the attention and felt I was experiencing my first taste of freedom, wondering how far that would actually take me, I still had strict limitations as to how far I could go, mainly because my mom was always with us, taking care of me, making sure I didn't get into any trouble, doing my laundry, washing and ironing my shirts, and generally offering me ironclad moral support. Justin's mom was there too, because he and I were still under eighteen. The record company paid them to chaperone us wherever we went (which, of course, we actually paid for as a recoupable charge against our earnings). Whenever my mother or Justin's mom expressed any concern over the fast pace of our lives, Lou was quick to soothe their fears, telling them not to worry. "Your kids are going to make *so much money!*"

Every few months we'd get a break, which meant an opportunity to fly back to Orlando. While we all loved the high energy of our European adventure, it was still a relief to get off the endless career turntable, if only for a few days. To be able to walk around neighborhood malls in America, hear a language I knew how to speak, and not have to worry about anything I had to do was so great. I had almost forgotten how much fun it was to be a teenager.

Thankfully, we were still completely unknown in

the States—*now I loved that fact*. Living and performing in Europe was like our day job—the greatest job in
the world—but being home was like one big summer
vacation.

Funny enough, none of my friends believed that I had
been doing anything in Europe, let alone that I was now a
member of one of the biggest musical acts over there. The
reason was, our album still hadn't been released in the
States, and radio and even MTV couldn't have cared less
about what was going on in the European world of teenage entertainment. I'd show my friends pictures of myself
onstage, with all the madness surrounding us, and they'd
laugh it off as some kind of joke or exaggeration. In a way
the laugh was on them, because I knew that these were
probably the last days I could ever spend this way: young,
anonymous, able to hang out with friends, being myself
in a crowd and having a great time.

For the last time I was one of them. In a way I was
witnessing the preparations for the death of my own
innocence.

All too soon we returned to Germany and resumed
our relentless touring schedule, which took us once
again all over Europe—including London, France,

and Spain—and even branched out to Asia. One night we did a show in Budapest, and Vince DiGiorgio had heard about *NSYNC and flew a couple of his people over from Germany to see us perform. Afterward he came backstage and said he wanted to release us on RCA in America. (RCA was an affiliate of our label BMG.) "America," he declared enthusiastically, "is ready for you."

We weren't quite sure what he meant by that; we felt that we'd been ready for America forever. But the one thing we wanted more than anything was to make it in the States, and because of that we were all excited about an American release.

Even more so since the Backstreet Boys continued to be a kind of musical thorn in our sides. In Europe we were too often unfavorably compared to them, called "Backstreet Boys wannabes" in the rock press. At times we felt like BMG's redheaded stepchild. We didn't know the Backstreet Boys and they didn't know us, which I think was done purposely by Lou Pearlman—we were kept separated, "enemies," as it were, even though we were all living in the same German cities, so we wouldn't become friends and ruin the so-called rivalry. Lou and his people would constantly tell us stories about what "those guys" had supposedly said, and it would make us mad, and then they would tell them things that we'd supposedly said. They would say to us, for example, "Kevin [Richardson] doesn't like you all because of so and so. . . ." And to them, "Lance hates the way you sing. . . ." The situation seemed engineered so that we would continue to keep our distance. Another consequence of this was that we never all got together to talk about the money we were making — or, more accurately, weren't making. Whenever we'd run into the Backstreet Boys, we'd be very cordial but always cold (though later we became more friendly).

And you know, there was some truth in what the press said, even though they didn't know the inside story. *NSYNC always got the feeling from Lou that we were indeed his stepchildren. Even though we had a number one album that had gone platinum, we always felt like we came in second in Lou's eyes. We could never top the Backstreet Boys for a very logical as well as emotional reason: They were his firstborn and therefore his sentimental favorite.

Families are families, wherever they are and however they operate.

Early in 1998 RCA agreed to A&R (find songs and

producers, and record) any new recordings we did and release a new version of our first overseas album (the best of the original German version plus a couple of new songs for America) in the States. We were incredibly happy and excited because that meant we were going to be released back home before the Backstreet Boys. We wanted to be the first American boy band, if you will, and for a change have the Backstreet Boys be known as "*NSYNC wannabes."

However, this was not what was going to happen. Although Backstreet Boys were signed to Jive Records, they were still managed by Lou Pearlman and Transcon, which maintained control of that band's destiny. In the end, our first American-released album, which was finished, was not released until after theirs came out. We had to wait to be second. So no matter how successful we would become, they would always be able to say they got there first. Sure enough, when our album was finally released (and we thought it was superior to theirs), it wasn't (and we weren't) taken as seriously as they were. We wanted to show America what we could do. Although we started off with this handicap, when "I Want You Back" was released, followed by "Tearin' Up My Heart," the Backstreet Boys really had no answer,

and we finally began to get airplay on American radio
stations.

I'll never forget the first time I heard one of our records played back home on the radio. It was on XL 106.7 in Orlando, during a "Battle of the Bands" program. I couldn't believe how great it was to hear *NSYNC coming out of the speakers. It made me feel like I was on top of the world.

In order to keep the momentum going Lou booked us into a lot of local clubs across the country. Unlike in Europe, the stages were really small and often had poles in the middle. More than once during our show, because of our intricate choreography we'd run smack into those poles. In one club in Texas they only gave us four cordless mikes and one with a cord. We had to continually toss the mikes back and forth to the guy on the end. After Europe it was a real case of more dues-paying.

Not long after that, we got a call from the Disney Channel. They wanted us to do a special for their cable station. This was the first time they were going to devote a whole hour to one group, and they wanted that group to be us.

We did the show at their Orlando studios, a well-produced live concert with individual band-member interviews dispersed throughout. The last part proved crucial, because it gave names and personalities to the individual members, making us real people rather than just stick figures on a stage. After two years spent getting our act together in Germany, we had our stuff down pat, plus we were so pumped, we were on fire that night. The combination was a good one, and we put on one of the best shows since we'd started singing together as a group. It proved so popular that Disney aired it consistently for six months, and it was the single biggest factor in turning us into American pop superstars. Kids just couldn't get enough of us. It was, at the time, the biggest Disney special ever.

For us it meant no more clubs, no more bumping into poles. Because of that show, every young person in America with access to cable finally knew who *NSYNC was!

Our videos jumped into heavy rotation on MTV, and in 1998 we appeared live on a brand-new show called *TRL* (*Total Request Live*), which was fast becoming the must-see daily teen program, broadcast live from MTV's Times Square studio. We became fairly regular visitors, and as a result every time we released a single it blew sky-high onto the charts. We had one hit after another, each bigger than the one before. We became the face of the new MTV generation.

As time went on, we wanted to focus on improving the quality of our music. Our continuing success both worldwide and in the States convinced us we were legitimate artists, not just a novelty. We had number one albums everywhere, we'd sold millions of copies of our debut album, and we wanted to produce great and lasting music.

By fall 1998 *NSYNC was arguably the most popular contemporary group in America, having sold about three million copies of our first album and another million of a Christmas album (eventually more than two million of that one were sold, a huge number for a "specialty" album). Every girl between eight and sixteen knew our names, our faces, our favorite colors, etc. Yet, believe it or not, every one of us was still dirt poor. For all the massive revenue we had produced for our label and our management, according to Lou Pearlman we were still deep in the red of the "recoupable" payback hole, and because of it profits were somewhere at the other side of that far-away rainbow. Each member of the band had to make do living off a thirty-five-dollar per diem. That's right:

thirty-five dollars a day and that was it. We hadn't as yet seen a single royalty paycheck of any kind. Not only that, *NSYNC merchandise was selling like crazy—*NSYNC T-shirts, *NSYNC toys, every product you could think of. Lou had smartly farmed us out to a big merchandiser who knew how to maximize this kind of thing, so not only was every penny Lou made from it pure income, he kept one hundred percent of every penny because of the way he was accounting for it. We were contractually entitled to half, however our money was subject to commission, and all of it was subject to the seemingly bottomless "recoupment."

In other words, he got everything. We got nothing.

In November 1998 Jan Bolz, the president of BMG Ariola Munich and a great guy, came to see us in Las Vegas, where on Thanksgiving weekend we were appearing on a televised Billboard Awards show. My mom was there, along with Justin's mom, Lynn, and several other *NSYNC family members. Because it was a holiday, a lot of us wanted to be with our loved ones, so we flew them all in.

It was a rare thing for everyone and their families to be all together. After the show we got to talking about things.

At one point my mom asked Jan in a good-natured way if her boy was ever going to get paid. After all, she told Jan, we had been on his label for three years and had not as yet seen so much as a penny. Jan smiled and calmly repeated the standard corporate mantra, a tune we had become quite familiar with, that first the band had to recoup all the money that had been spent to make the sensation that we had become.

"Yeah," I said, jumping in. "But we've already sold fifteen million albums! How much could we have possibly spent against that?" No one from the record company or from Lou's group could tell us why we were still in debt.

"Not to worry," Jan said, after what I would call a lot of double-talk, "because this is the day you've been waiting for." He had actually planned his appearance as part of a big surprise for us: the first actual check presentation to the boys of *NSYNC. What can I say, we were beside ourselves with anticipation. We had no idea how much we were going to get, but we figured that after all this time and all the albums we'd sold and all the concerts we'd done, there had to be a lot of money waiting for us.

Jan had arranged it so that this was to be a closed ceremony in one of the private rooms at a fancy steak house. There were no press or other media around. It was a private moment for him to reward us for all our hard work and loyalty. Lou was there too, and both of them made brief ceremonial speeches, while I sat there with the others, smiling and trying to calculate my cut of the deal. *Let's see, fifteen million albums worldwide, all those tours in Europe and in the States, hit singles, TV specials, a huge Christmas album, tons of merchandise . . .* I thought that maybe after all that "recouping," we'd be entitled to, say, two or three hundred thousand dollars? That would certainly do it for me. It crossed my mind that it could even be more than that, but I didn't want to be greedy. That would certainly be enough to make us feel we had actually accomplished something special. I couldn't help chuckling to myself as I thought about going from thirty-five dollars a day to having half a million dollars in the bank.

After what seemed like an eternity, the checks were finally passed out by Lou Pearlman. I looked at mine and my eyes widened. I stared at it in shocked disbelief and read the amount over and over again to make sure I was seeing what I was seeing. I was holding in my hand a check for twenty-five thousand dollars, the sum total they claimed I'd made since I'd joined the band.

I felt as if someone had walked up to me with a big

smile and slapped me hard across the face. I had thought of Lou as a member of the family, but I felt that I'd been screwed over. My trust had been unlimited, and now I had learned a cruel lesson. I knew I would never be able to completely rely on anyone in this business again, no matter how nice they seemed. I had to grow up now, really fast, and leave my surrogate father behind.

I wanted to make the point that I got it—I had thought I'd earn a lot of money but I didn't, and I could still feel it in my most tender spot. My heart. I would never allow something like this to happen again. My first question from then on, with any stranger, no matter how much I liked them or was attracted to them, was going to be, *What do they want out of me?* My guard was up, and it would never go completely down again.

Without saying a word I tore up the check, threw the pieces up in the air, and left the room.

In December I was still hot over what had gone down in Las Vegas. Finally, JC's parents and my parents decided to get together and call JC's uncle, Phil Baker-Shenk, a lawyer who worked with a major New York–based entertainment litigator by the name of Helene Freeman. Helene said she would look at the production contract, one of several deals the band had with Pearlman. Halfway through she called to tell us, "Congratulations. This is the worst contract in music history." She said we needed some real help and put us in touch with a transactional entertainment attorney, Adam Ritholz, who had a great reputation within the music industry.

After Adam pored over every word of the contract, he wrote an opinion letter to us. Adam then agreed to meet with JC and me and our parents in New York City. We all flew in for it. I liked him a lot and agreed with JC that he should send his letter to the other guys. At that point we officially retained him as our lawyer. After reading our production contract, Adam sent a letter to Lou Pearlman's lawyer demanding copies of any and all other contracts involving us and the companies Lou had set up.

Because of that, two amazing things happened. First, shortly after Adam sent the letter, each member of the band received a check for fifty thousand dollars. I think Jan Bolz, along with everyone else involved with *NSYNC at the business level, felt that Lou was not acting in our best interests, but none of them wanted to kill their piece of this fabulous golden goose. The bottom line from everyone was the same: Work out your differences and continue with Lou. After all, they said, he was the one who'd brought us

Lou to renegotiate a new and better deal. He worked for a long time with Lou's lawyer, Larry Rudolph (later on Britney Spears's manager), and made it very clear we weren't asking for the moon. All we wanted was a better deal, and so Adam made them a proposal.

After a little back-and-forth, Lou's bottom line, via Larry Rudolph, was a simple, no-two-ways-about-it no.

Despite the fact that he had repeatedly told Adam and us he would give us anything we wanted, Lou absolutely refused to renegotiate anything. Instead he insisted he had us tied to him with ironclad contracts that called for four more *NSYNC albums (not counting the Christmas album we had done, which was a one-off, or one-time special deal) with no time limitations, and he wanted them all before he would consider any renegotiating.

Moreover, he had created us in the form of a company—*NSYNC, Inc. That made him a one-sixth partner in the band, he insisted, in addition to all his other holdings in the band in both his own name and that of his company. So he got one-sixth of all monies from touring. He was also receiving several types of payment, either personally or through Transcon, including more than half of our record royalties and merchandise earnings, and a 20-percent commission on all touring.

to the big dance, and it's always best to leave with the one you came with.

Things were really getting complicated. To us, the guys in the group, while the new check came at a time when we all really needed another influx of cash, we also felt that Lou must have been ripping us off. Adam received another packet of agreements signed by Lou in his self-appointed capacity as the "sixth member of the group." Nobody except Lou had ever seen all of them together before, and they were, of course, outlandishly one-sided, giving him everything but *NSYNC's proverbial kitchen sink (although maybe that was in there too, in which case we'd likely have had to pay to wash our own dishes). Things were worse than even Helene had initially thought.

When we next met with Adam, he decided to get in touch with Lou's attorneys to try to hammer out a more acceptable set of agreements. Lou said that that was fine with him and that he would do anything in his power to keep us happy. We were his boys, he said proudly, "and we are all in this together."

And that was it: The tiger had smiled and bared his fangs. The fight was on.

Adam thought it might still be possible to convince

Essentially, he was taking his own cut as well as commissioning himself and Transcon out of our share. He was getting it from both ends, and we were the ones paying for all of it before we could see a single penny. Three little letters, one little word—"net"—made the difference that amounted to millions in his pocket and out of ours.

He also owned 100 percent of the publishing rights and there was a consulting agreement between Transcon and *NSYNC, Inc., where in exchange for loans and business counseling he received an additional 10 percent. (A typical manager's fee is a straight 15 to 20 percent.) Whatever paltry sum was left over was to be divided among the five of us.

In other words, according to Lou, we had legally signed away the vast majority of any income we would ever earn while Lou Pearlman's various companies benefited tremendously.

We soon found out that the Backstreet Boys were also going through a nightmare with Lou and Transcon. They had previously signed a similar deal. Adam discovered this when he reviewed the agreements and saw that Lou's lawyer had mistakenly left in the name Backstreet Boys instead of *NSYNC in some of the agreements. Wisely, the Backstreet Boys had gotten themselves lawyers as well.

At some point, we got word that we should fly down to Orlando. There was a showdown meeting scheduled that required all parties to be present. None of us in the group had much hope at this point, as we kept getting the same message over and over again from Adam—that Lou was continuing to offer us financial scraps and that he had no intention of making any real changes.

Still, it was difficult for me to believe that he wasn't going to budge, even a little. I was going to have to hear that from Lou himself before I would accept it as the truth.

The meeting was long and painful and a complete disappointment for us. Each member of our legal team presented our arguments again, calmly and quietly. Lou listened, then proceeded to posture and pontificate, demonstrating a particularly rich abundance of self-righteousness and entitlement, speaking down to us as if we were little children. He was being totally obnoxious, there is just no other way to say it, as he gave us the same stale rationale that he had used since the beginning of these negotiations. He explained yet again that we were nothing but a business to him, that if he didn't get a decent enough return on his investment from us, he might as well take all the money he had put into making us who we had become and invest instead in the stock market.

So that was it. I was a commodity along with the other guys. Something to make money off of, nothing more and maybe even a whole lot less.

At the end of the meeting he gave us some time to talk everything over among ourselves. He provided a room barely big enough for all of us to fit into, let alone sit and discuss the situation: a storage room for his office supplies and copying-machine equipment. Adam now told us we had only two choices: We could walk out right then and there and he would stay behind and try to continue to renegotiate with Lou, or we could come back to Lou one last time, united, with one final offer.

We thought about it and agreed to make one last proposal to Lou, which, frankly, even our own lawyer thought was crazy. We were willing to offer a full 25 percent of all our gross earned income for the remainder of our contract until those last four albums were finished, no matter how long it took. That included all monies from touring, records, merchandise, endorsements—all of it. In return we wanted everything to go directly through RCA rather than Transcon. And we wanted Johnny Wright, who worked for Lou, to receive a management commission (okay to come out of our end, which we thought was fair) but nothing more. To us, the key was in the accounting.

We figured RCA would not screw us the way Lou had.

Lou laughed in our faces when he heard the offer. He never even made a counterproposal. Instead he harped on how ungrateful we were. It was JC who stood up first, took a deep breath, and spoke. "Thank you for your hospitality, Lou. It's been great. I've got a plane to catch. See ya." With that, he walked out. I did the same—got up, paid my respects, and left. Right behind me came Justin, Joey, and Chris. And that was it, the last time any of us ever spoke face-to-face with Lou Pearlman. We had held out for the longest time, not believing that Lou was willingly giving us the royal shaft. Now, finally, the pain in our asses told us we knew better.

Nothing changed, and as usual we were on top of the world and practically broke, unable to afford a cab to take us down off the high road. At that point Adam and Helene decided there was no other choice: They had to get us out of the deal somehow. Adam went back and pored over the contracts, looking for a way out. Then, miraculously, at the end of May, after a negotiation that was going nowhere, he found one. The contract said that from the day we finished our album, Transcon had exactly one year to release our album in the United States or we would have the right to find ourselves a separate American label independent of Pearlman and Transcon. Pearlman had indeed found us a label, RCA, which was a division of BMG, a German company. But they didn't release our album within a year, and that ultimately became our escape clause. Without getting overly technical, the way it was explained to me was that usually when there is a commitment in a contract, in this case for an American release, there is a thirty-day limitation on the right of the other party to give notice of a breach. What Adam was saying to us was that this contract did not limit the timing of our right to give notice, and so we could use the one-year clause to be free from the clutches of Transcon and Lou Pearlman.

Adam then notified Transcon in writing that our contract with BMG was terminated. Accordingly, we were free and clear. If RCA wanted to re-sign us, fine, we were willing to listen. Otherwise we were walking.

To be honest, everyone, including us, thought Adam was a little nuts. *Hits* magazine even did a piece where they effectively said that Adam either had the biggest balls in the industry or several screws seriously loose. In other words, no one thought he stood a chance of making that provision stick. The universal advice was that we should continue to try to renegotiate.

Adam, meanwhile, continued to talk with Lou all summer. Lou said he wanted to be reasonable but needed us to go out on the road during the negotiations so we wouldn't lose the momentum we had built up in America. That made sense to Adam and us and we agreed, which is why throughout the summer and fall of 1999, *NSYNC played more than one hundred concerts for an agreed-upon salary, even as our legal team continued to fight for a new and better deal.

We decided to go out with the Ain't No Stoppin' Us Now tour even though we knew that Lou was going to continue to benefit from it, mostly because we didn't want to disappoint our fans. *NSYNC's dispute was with Lou Pearlman, not the fans who wanted to see us, and we couldn't see how depriving them would be of any benefit to our own internal battles.

In any event, when August arrived and there was no new deal, Adam began listening to other offers.

Bob Jamieson, RCA's president, couldn't believe we would actually walk. He was in fact more than willing to renegotiate with us. The thought that the label could conceivably lose *NSYNC was a nightmare to him. However, Strauss Zelnick, the head of BMG and Jamieson's boss, wouldn't let him loose on this. Zelnick was prepared to rely on his contract with Pearlman and wasn't interested in renegotiation.

Adam then began talking to both Clive Calder's Jive Records and people at all the major labels. Most of them expressed the same reservation: that signing us would only land them in the deep end of a legal quagmire. Clive Calder, a sophisticated yet down-to-earth, unostentatious South African, soft-spoken but very effective, still wanted the band for his independent Jive Records label.

When Adam brought us the offer from Jive, we talked among ourselves for a while about making that deal before we actually signed. Jive, after all, was the longtime distributor of the Backstreet Boys, and we weren't sure we wanted to be just another boy band on Clive's roster. Adam kept telling us that they were just another band and every label would have someone on their roster who was going to be competitive with us. Finally, when we realized that Jive was a great label for us, that they were independent and knew how to market music, we decided to accept their offer. We could very well become even bigger than we already were. What's more, Clive was willing to deal with whatever legal battle Lou would surely put up.

Even as all the craziness was going on, with stories in the newspaper and our lawyers and the other side lobbing metaphorical letter bombs at each other, we went back into Johnny's studio in Orlando to start work on our new record!

At the end of September, just before the 1999 MTV Music Awards broadcast, we put our signatures on the contract with Jive Records. RCA didn't want us to make the deal, but it was too late. Three weeks after we signed we were hit with a lawsuit intended to void the Jive deal.

Fast-forward to November and a hearing to decide whether BMG and Transcon could stop Jive from putting out our new record. It was to be a one-day hearing, and now it was do or die time, the day of reckoning. It was either all over and *NSYNC was history—if the decision went against us, we were prepared to break up the band rather than continue with Lou Pearlman—or we were finally going to be allowed to continue free and clear with Jive, minus the sweatshop contract we had been tied to before.

We all dressed up and sat in a row, having been told by Adam not to say a word, no matter what took place. Every so often I'd look out of the corner of my eye and see my mom and Justin's mom holding hands because they were so nervous.

Then, to our delight, the judge really pulled Lou Pearlman's pants down. The best part was when Lou's new litigation lawyer was ranting and raving about Lou owning *NSYNC, insisting that Lou *was* *NSYNC because by contract he was the sixth member and could put whomever he wanted in the group. The judge looked at Lou as if in disbelief and said, "So you're telling me that *Mr. Pearlman* is *NSYNC, and these five guys over here my daughter has a poster of on her wall are *not* *NSYNC?" Lou turned red as a beet. I thought he was going to explode!

The judge warned the plaintiffs that they should consider settling with us and fast, because they wouldn't want to hear her ruling on their request for a temporary restraining order. That was the end and everyone knew it. We walked out of the courtroom and there were hundreds of fans waiting for us, cheering our victory. It was almost a year to the day since I had torn up that twenty-five-thousand-dollar check. Thanksgiving was two days away, and this year we had a lot to be grateful for! Our lawyers hunkered down for a few days and eventually worked out a settlement.

We couldn't wait to go back out on the road. We went on a world tour that took us well into the new year. One day we were in London in a taxicab, in town to do *Top of the Pops*, talking about what we should put on our first album for Jive. "There's no strings on us anymore—we're like Pinocchio," I said, and Chris said, "Yeah! No strings attached!" We all looked at each other and knew immediately that we had found a concept for the album. It all fell together quickly after that. We could see the stage show in front of our eyes, *NSYNC hanging like puppets and then being liberated—or, more accurately, liberating ourselves. We were clicking. When we got back to the States, we went into the studio and got it all down. We got some major-league writers and producers to work with us, including Max Martin, Teddy Riley, and Richard Marx, to help us record the rest of our new songs. For the first time it felt like we were nobody's puppets anymore.

As for me, the sense of liberation that I had been nurturing in my soul took a giant step toward becoming a reality. I had managed to shed one of the most repressive relationships I had ever had in my life.

Even though this was our second American album, to us *No Strings Attached* felt like the first true *NSYNC album. March 21, 2000, the day *No Strings Attached* was released, was the day we were finally allowed to grow up.

* * *

It's difficult to describe the impact that *No Strings Attached* had. There hadn't been an all-new *NSYNC album in more than two years, and our fans were chomping at the bit. *No Strings Attached* exploded onto the charts like a champagne bottle that had been shaken up before the cork was finally allowed to pop.

No album in the history of music has ever done what *No Strings Attached* did. It sold more than 1.2 million copies its very first day of release, and by the end of that first week we hit the two and a half million mark. What was especially sweet to us was that the Backstreet Boys had released their album a year earlier and had broken all first-week sales. We knew everyone was watching to see how we would do on our new label and if we could catch them. If we didn't, no matter how successful we were, everyone would see us as having failed, still in the shadow of the Backstreet Boys. All the pressure made passing them that much greater to us.

No Strings Attached eventually passed the ten-million sales mark—the extremely rare Diamond level—selling more than eleven million copies in the United States alone. With the music business being what it is today, there is a pretty good chance our numbers will never be matched, an achievement I am so proud to have been a part of.

Not that it was all smooth sailing. We were on *Saturday Night Live* that week, to kick off the album, and during our spot I broke my ankle! For the next two months I had to dance on tour as it healed.

Once the album took off, we did every show imaginable—Leno, Rosie, all of it—as we were determined, now that we had taken over the top spot, to stay there forever. With Rosie in particular, I'd always thought to myself, *If we ever do her show, I'll know that we've finally made it big in America.* And we finally did—both her show and arrive.

Doing that album and the success of its release made this one of the most glorious times of my life.

Now all I had to do was figure out how to be as true to myself in real life as my voice sounded on those songs.

Chapter Four

Three years, two albums, and countless concerts after we
had won our freedom from Lou Pearlman, *NSYNC
was the most popular band in the world. Our fans
stood behind us through all the infighting and followed us to Jive Records. Here I was, Lance Bass from
Mississippi, rock star! Okay, okay, *pop* star. It was like
that old song goes: I was sitting on top of the world.
Screaming girls! Screaming boys! *Screaming mothers of
screaming girls and boys!*

It felt like it was one big party every time we stepped
onto a stage. Girls, especially, would do *anything* to get
backstage or find out what hotel we were staying in. They

would camp out in our lobby and constantly try to sneak into our rooms, pretending to be delivering something, or banging on the door until their fingers bled while tears ran down their faces. It was a ridiculous, delightful madness. Some of the guys took the offerings like kings at a sacrificial ritual. I, of course, was less interested in the girls than I was in the excitement of it all. Knowing that if I wanted to I could have had dozens, no, make that hundreds, maybe thousands of girls, was all I really needed. Acceptance at the fantasy level was for the moment quite satisfying. I was not ready to show my hand and let the others in on my true sexuality.

The first time I allowed myself to have any kind of sexual encounter with a guy was in Chicago, in 2000 during the Celebrity tour. I took my friend and producing partner Wendy Thorlakson with me to an after-show party for *Mamma Mia!* There I met a cast member I found extremely attractive, and I could tell he was interested in me, too. In a bold gesture I managed to invite him back to my hotel room without anybody knowing about it. It was tricky and dangerous, but I pulled it off. From then on I knew I was going to be able to come into myself. I think being on the road, away from home, had a lot to do with my taking this kind of

My mom, Diane; my sister, Stacy (age twelve); me (age nine); and my dad, Jim

Me at age three.

I loved attending space camp at age eight. Note my NASA visor.

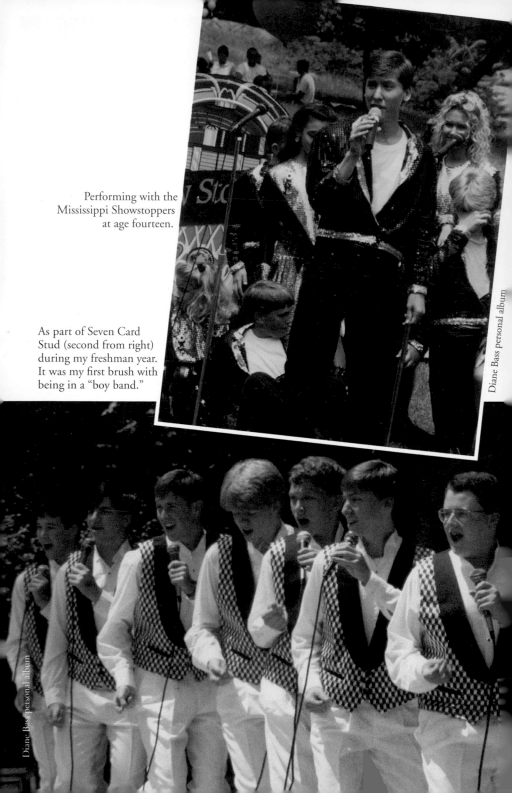

Performing with the
Mississippi Showstoppers
at age fourteen.

As part of Seven Card
Stud (second from right)
during my freshman year.
It was my first brush with
being in a "boy band."

My mom took this very first photo of *NSYNC together at Planet Hollywood in October 1995.

A party in Orlando to celebrate our very first gold record

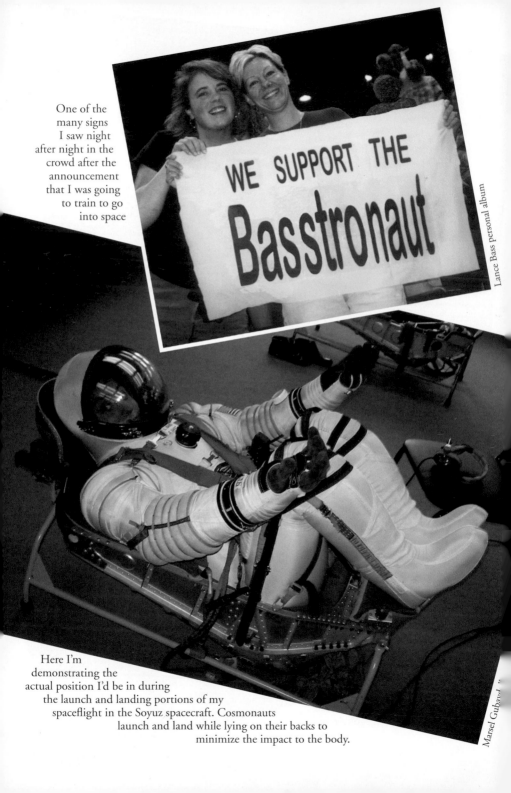

One of the many signs I saw night after night in the crowd after the announcement that I was going to train to go into space

WE SUPPORT THE Basstronaut

Lance Bass personal album

Here I'm demonstrating the actual position I'd be in during the launch and landing portions of my spaceflight in the Soyuz spacecraft. Cosmonauts launch and land while lying on their backs to minimize the impact to the body.

Marsel Gubaid ''

My official cosmonaut photo. The shoot took me by surprise. The schedule
was written in Russian, and I thought I was going to a photography class.

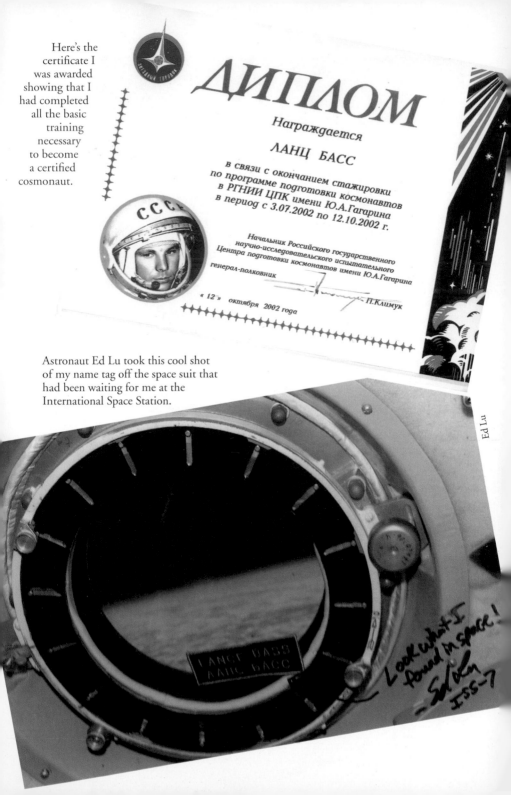

Here's the certificate I was awarded showing that I had completed all the basic training necessary to become a certified cosmonaut.

ДИПЛОМ

Награждается

ЛАНЦ БАСС

в связи с окончанием стажировки
по программе подготовки космонавтов
в РГНИИ ЦПК имени Ю.А.Гагарина
в период с 3.07.2002 по 12.10.2002 г.

Начальник Российского государственного
научно-исследовательского испытательного
Центра подготовки космонавтов имени Ю.А.Гагарина
генерал-полковник

« 12 » октября 2002 года   П.Климук

Astronaut Ed Lu took this cool shot of my name tag off the space suit that had been waiting for me at the International Space Station.

Ed Lu

Look what I found in space!
—Ed Lu
ISS-7

Running with the Olympic Torch in Newport Beach, California, for the 2002 Winter Games with my manager, Cindy Owen. This was one of the greatest thrills of my life.

Diane Bass personal album

Little did we know, this photo, taken July 20, 2003, at the Challenge for the Children Charity Game in Orlando, would be the last photo taken of the five of us together.

Courtesy of Challenge for the Children: Dean Ray & Kevin Mazur

Celebrating my twenty-eighth birthday with two of my best friends—my assistant, Lisa Delcampo, and Wendy Thorlakson

Tony Dimiao

© Ron Davis

Joey is truly my best friend.

risk, but, hey, I was young and having fun and wanted to live my life.

Not that there weren't some close calls. One time when I was at home, I threw a big party, and Joey walked into my home office, where I was alone with a guy, sitting very close to him. Fortunately, nothing as yet had happened between this guy and me, but Joey simply chose to literally look the other way. He smiled, said, "What the f**k?" turned around, and left. Later on he told me he knew right then and there I was gay, but that he really didn't care one way or the other. Or as he put it, "Nobody in the band really gives a shit. My friendship with you has nothing to do with your sexual preferences." And then he added that he was worried what my mother would say if she ever found out, and that my father would probably kill me. I told him to get in line for that one.

Chicago was by far the rare exception rather than the norm. For the most part I went with the general frenzy of being in *NSYNC, enjoying the euphoria of this very real unreality. Whenever we took the stage, I'd look out at thousands and thousands of packed people, all cheering for *NSYNC and screaming over every move we made. It was like being at a nightly coronation, like having your best childhood dream come true a thousand times better than you could ever imagine. Our fans made us feel that we were the reason they were living, that's how strong and visceral it was. And always, after about ten minutes, the sweet odor of teenage desire would waft up to the stage. We could see it in the eyes of the kids down front, and we could smell it from the last row in the back.

I didn't know what pop adulation was all about until I joined *NSYNC. And our fans were the best; they were totally connected to us. They knew everything about us and the show we were going to put on even before we took the stage or played a single note. When they'd see us do our thing onstage, they could barely handle it.

There was no way, especially since we were still kids ourselves, to properly prepare us for any of that. I can understand why some teen idols have such a hard time growing up. Inevitably, the illusion and the real thing start to blend into each other—you *are* the greatest, you *are* perfect, you can do anything you want. No matter what, your fans will accept and love you. You can have sex with anybody and everybody; *you can do no wrong*. It's like a perfect teenage love affair with millions of people trying to push their way to the front of the line, where you are standing, smiling, waiting to see who wins the prize, and the prize is you.

We always had one eye on the next step—what did we have to do and what would come out of it? We never lost sight of that, but we also knew that once a show was over for the night, we were a bunch of young guys who wanted to have some fun. Everything else could wait until the morning.

The wildest and most exciting time was always the first day of whatever tour we were out on. It was usually the culmination of a month's rehearsal: learning the songs, learning the choreography, learning the special material. To try to keep the audiences as off balance as we could, we'd change the order of our songs right up until curtain. However, because ours was such a technical show, we were always worried that something was going to go wrong. Somehow, every first show of ours went off without a hitch, a testament to the amount of work we put in.

It was extremely hard to come down from all of that every night. I could hear the screaming of the audience in my head for hours after, and it energized me. Two hours on the stage, singing and dancing and sweating off ten pounds, gave me the biggest cardio rush of my life. Most times I couldn't get to sleep until early the next day; it would take that long to come down from the performing high. If we weren't going too far, I'd wait until we got to the next city before even trying to sleep. We'd be back in our bus while the backing band was playing the final notes of the show, already on the way to the next city. My clothes would be soaking wet, my microphone still attached to my head, and then I'd have to deal with the adrenaline rush that takes forever to go away. I'd eat all the worst foods imaginable—pizza, bread sticks, chips, all of which was fine because doing the kind of physical show we put on, I knew I would work it off.

With all our financial problems resolved, for the first time in my life I was not only doing something I really loved, but I was making a living from it as well. My only problem was the same one that I had had since I was a little boy. There was all this opportunity around and no chance for me to do anything about it. It was a strange irony. Back home I couldn't do anything because of my parents. Now I couldn't do anything because of the other guys in the band. Our image was rock solid; we were pop stars, and that meant we were perfect little models of make-out and other assorted acts of merriment—as long as they were between boys and girls. I feared what I always feared, that anything I might do for myself could hurt everyone around me. As much as I wanted to break out, I knew I couldn't. At least not yet.

It got so very lonely. Everyone around me had a girlfriend. I wanted so desperately to experience love like
everyone else, but I couldn't.

Still, everyone dreams of being successful at something
they love. My big dream had always been to one day make
enough money to take care of my entire family. That's why
as soon as the first big check cleared, I retired my dad from
his position as lab manager and hired my sister, Stacy, to
work for me. My dad's job had been really stressful, and
while my mom loved teaching, it was a very demanding
job that paid relatively little. I put them all in charge of my
website, my fan-based activities, and the Lance Bass Foundation (for children's causes), and I bought my parents and
my sister great houses in Mississippi. I was determined to
ensure that they would never have to worry about anything
in their lives again.

Touring had become my way of life. We had been out
on the road behind *No Strings Attached* for a solid year,
and then, after a brief hiatus, we began work on our next
album, *Celebrity*, a sort of progress report on what success
had done for and to us. With it the band took a step up
from being just a pop boy band to one capable of recording edgy, hard R&B dance music.

We each knew our place in the band, our designated role, which is why any changes from the so-called norm immediately stood out to us. The biggest had to do with Justin. On *No Strings Attached* JC had shared most of the leads, and he'd cowritten and coproduced a lot of the music. On *Celebrity* Justin took the lead, which was fine with the rest of us because no one could sing in that style better than he could. We were a tight unit and didn't feel threatened by this shift. As a result we had some of our biggest hits, including "Girlfriend," "Pop," and "Gone."

I knew that this time going back on the road I would need another "me," someone who could do everything I was too busy to do, an assistant who wasn't a total stranger so neither of us would feel uncomfortable. It was a luxury I felt I deserved.

I couldn't find the right person until one weekend I went back to Brandon, Mississippi, which is right next to Clinton, where I'd bought my parents their house, and I happened to run into Beth Flanagan, with whom I'd gone to high school. She was at the time in her last semester at Ole Miss (the University of Mississippi), majoring in marketing. I suddenly flashed on how Beth, who was always superorganized, could be just the person I was looking for. Not only was she capable of doing the job, but she'd be a touch of home closer to my own age while I was on the road.

I offered her a job and she accepted immediately. Once we started working together, she became like this great older sister, taking care of everything I needed. She'd run errands for me, go to the grocery, arrange tables for me at restaurants, and buy tickets at the movies — all the things I couldn't do for myself without causing a commotion wherever I went.

Among the many things Beth helped make happen was that at every one of our shows a child from the Make-a-Wish Foundation was there as our guest, escorted backstage to meet the band and have pictures taken. Beth always arranged all of that. She helped me organize my photo-taking and autograph-signing so that everyone got what they wanted.

And on the days I felt like doing nothing but sleeping in, chilling out, and hanging loose, Beth was great at making sure I was able to do exactly that without a lot of little things getting in the way and taking up time. Because of her I could stay curled up in bed until ten minutes before the car arrived to take us to our next airport. Sometimes getting me to make those pickups on time drove Beth nuts, but as I used to tell her with a grin on my face and a glass of milk in my hand, "A growing boy needs his sleep."

She also assisted me with some of the things I had agreed to handle as the band's business representative. We'd gotten together and voted on who we thought was the most business-oriented among us, and that turned out to be me. I didn't mind, as I have always had the kind of head for that sort of thing, along with a fair amount of tolerance and patience.

For the PopOdyssey tour we traveled on a total of twenty-four buses and ninety-two trucks, and three hundred people traveled with the band. It took five hundred people to set up the tour, five full days to set up each stage, and three thousand meals per city to feed our crew. We had a game room that followed us wherever we went, which was always stocked with pinball machines, scooters, and skateboards. We were like little kids, playing around and having fun until it was time to do the show. We'd get up around four in the afternoon, maybe a little earlier if we wanted to go do something, get to the venue by six, do our sound check, be on stage by nine, and before the backing band had finished we'd be back on the bus, soaked in sweat, off into the night. We'd

Of course, no road ever existed that didn't have some bumps, and ours had its share. We were no longer able to have anything like normal social lives or ordinary everyday fun. The only people we could be friends with now, besides each other, were people we spent the most time with, like the crew and the few close friends from back home we kept in touch with, who'd known us early on. Since I came from the rural Deep South, where home is the center of the universe, friends meant everything to me, and I wanted to keep my old prefame group of them together as much as possible. That was my thing.

Justin, meanwhile, was still dating Britney Spears, his former "sister" Mouseketeer. At the time she struck me as just this adorable little teenage girl at a perennial slumber party—staying up late and having lots of fun. She showed no signs of the turmoil she would eventually encounter, maybe because I felt she was so in love with Justin that she thought it was going to last forever. I knew it wouldn't. Justin already had a great love in his life—his career. He wanted to be a star, and no girl, no matter how great, was going to be able to distract him from that for more than a night or two between trips to the center of the spotlight. But as I said, they were an awfully cute couple, and she seemed like the perfect girl-

be so pumped that we couldn't even think about sleep for hours. Luckily there were showers on the buses so we could get cleaned up on the way to wherever we were going next.

Toward the end of the PopOdyssey tour we hit the absolute zenith of touring: every pop star's dream shows. We did three consecutive nights at Giants Stadium in front of seventy thousand–plus highly enthusiastic fans. The crowd went crazy as surging energy filled the place with sheer pandemonium. We pulled the kinds of crowds that once only the Rolling Stones and Bruce Springsteen could have generated in that venue.

There was a point in our show, during "God Must Have Spent a Little More Time on You," when all five of us stood on stage and were suddenly elevated by these platforms. They slowly lifted us ten, fifteen, twenty feet into the air. There was nothing like the feeling of looking over the entire audience, so high above them, so high above the world, as they cheered for us. Then, slowly, as the song ended, we were lowered back to the stage level—down to earth, as it were. Looking back now, that moment was the perfect metaphor for the band: exciting, a little dangerous, high-flying, a great ride on the way up, but one that sooner or later had to come back down.

* * *

friend, especially when she wore her pajamas and hung out with the boys.

Joey, my bus mate, he of the smelly socks and smellier farts, lover of all things porn, was more bark than bite, although he was the biggest flirt in the world (I think the porn kept him safe and sane). He could be a real pain in the ass, but so could I. We were like brothers, and that's what brothers are for, right? I traveled with lots of pets—including chinchillas and a ferret named Dirk. It got pretty funky in there, I guess that's the reason no one else wanted to share a bus with us (except Joey's brother, who occasionally came along for the ride, and my sister, who was oblivious to almost everything, having grown up with me as a brother). Besides, the other guys—including Joey—spent most of their off-time with girlfriends.

That was another reason I was grateful to have Beth around. If the others were wondering why I wasn't having my share of "fun," at least I had a woman in my presence; that helped me not completely stick out like a sore thumb. I had dated a few girls by now—I suppose it's inevitable in these surroundings—but in my heart I knew where my emotional reality was. It wouldn't have helped anything and more likely would have severely hurt us if I'd been found out at the height of *NSYNC's popularity.

We had worked long and hard to make it, and I couldn't risk that, not just for my own sake but for the rest of the guys in the band. So I kept my private life private and quietly went along with the publicity machine that always had us hooking up with girls. If that's what it took, then that's what it took.

After all this time, touring and all the between-shows drudgery that went with it became a bit monotonous, but I had no major complaints and neither did anyone else in the band. We had fought long and hard to get to where we were, we had proved that we could do it, and now we wanted to celebrate by showing the world just how good we thought we really were. Before this tour was over we would have played live for more than a million people and by my count I would have signed thousands and thousands of autographs. I loved every minute of it, because I still enjoyed performing more than anything else. I felt most comfortable in my life when I was onstage having a blast. The very thing I love about music is what *NSYNC was all about.

Eventually, however, I did find that I wanted more of a sense of myself as an individual. It was the beginning of my trying to establish who I really was outside of the defining context of the group. I thought about it for a long time and finally decided to try to get involved on my own in the film and television industry. My goal was to use my success with *NSYNC to open up new doors of opportunity. I had no idea that the other guys in the band were thinking the very same thing.

Somewhere along the way, on impulse (or maybe because I just couldn't stand the charade any longer), on an off—that is, non-performing—night, I decided to fly back to Orlando by myself and surprise a friend of mine, whom I'll call Scott. Well, in truth Scott was more than just a friend. We had shared something special, and every so often I was able to get away and meet with him, wherever he was. Without any of the others knowing, he had become my private escape from the reality of *NSYNC. We had first met in Orlando and that's where I wanted to be now. I flew in on a private plane and got in a little before midnight. Just before we started our final descent, I decided to give Scott a heads-up. "Guess what," I said. "I'm on my way to see you!"

"Oh," he said. I heard something in his voice that didn't sound quite right. I asked him if I was interrupting something, and he brushed the question off, never really answering it. Instead he said, "Look, I'll pick you up at the airport."

Right after I landed I called Scott's cell phone to make sure he was there and was sent immediately to voice mail. *Oh, great,* I thought to myself. I tried it again and the same thing happened. I retrieved my luggage and sat for thirty minutes at the pickup area waiting for Scott, who never showed. I tried his phone again, several times, and finally, after I'd already called a cab, he picked up. "Where the heck are you?" I asked.

"Sorry," he said, "I fell asleep on the couch."

Okay. Even though I knew I shouldn't have, I bought it. I canceled the cab and waited for him to show up. He came by and we went back to his apartment. He was cool, but something seemed wrong to me, and I couldn't shake it. Finally, I just flat-out asked what was going on.

He told me he'd been tied up with a girl.

"What girl?"

"Oh, just someone who works with me." I'd heard her name before and knew she had a big crush on him. I wondered why Scott hadn't just come out and told me that in the first place. And then I thought, *Wait.* "Were you having sex with her while I was trying to get you on the phone?"

He hesitated and then said, "Yeah, I was."

That's when I knew that whatever we had was over. I was crushed, but I tried to understand. I figured this was the time in his life when he needed to be experimental. It wouldn't be right if I tried to stop that. After all, this was my experimental time as well.

After it was over, it dawned on me that my feelings were so strong, the pain so deep, that this was the first real "relationship" I ever had.

But I also realized something else—that Scott was probably more important to me than I was to him. I guess I had always known that he was the kind of person who was never going to settle down. I'm long over what happened that night, but moments like that tend to stay inside of me for what feels like forever.

I first met Cindy Owen in October 2000 through Ron Davis, an L.A.-based celebrity photographer who was a mutual friend of ours. During an *NSYNC photo session Ron had told me all about her, and that she was based in Nashville and thought we should meet. At the time Cindy was an executive in her friend Reba McEntire's company, but after fifteen years she was ready to start her own management/consulting company. At the same time I was entertaining the idea of opening up my own artist-management firm based out of Nashville, where a lot of young talent seems to gather—and was interested in using Cindy to consult.

We met and hit it off beautifully. We got back together again the next night, and over dinner I told her, "I need a 'you.'" I asked her if she would consider taking me on as an individual to help me with my solo projects.

We formalized our working relationship in January 2002. A month later Cindy and I were both in Los Angeles taking meetings for several projects I was looking to get involved in during *NSYNC's upcoming six-month hiatus. I remember us leaving the William Morris offices in Beverly Hills together, high-fiving each other on the progress we were seeing for a film as well as a recurring role for me on one of the hit crime dramas.

Two weeks later Cindy received a fax from a television producer saying he had acquired the rights to seats on two separate space missions on a Russian Soyuz spacecraft and wanted to offer one of them to me. She immediately called my agent, John Ferriter at the William Morris Agency, to see if it was real and to check on the producer's validity. The opportunity was in fact real, and William

Morris had worked with the producer before on several projects. John knew about my long-standing dream to one day go into space.

One night in Orlando while I was having dinner with some friends my phone rang. It was Cindy. "Are you sitting down?" she asked.

"I am," I said.

She proceeded to tell me about the impending mission, the plan for the TV show, what would be expected of me as a cosmonaut, and what the training schedule would be. "Omigod," I said out loud. I couldn't believe what I was hearing. Ever since I was a little boy I had fantasized about going up in space and being an astronaut. For a brief second my eyes lit up with excitement! Then reality set in. I knew right then and there beyond a shadow of a doubt—*I was being "punk'd."* At the time Ashton Kutcher's MTV practical joke show was huge! He was having a blast catching celebrities off guard. For those of you who might not know, Ashton would pull pranks on celebrities and film them to air on a show he'd created and executive-produced called *Punk'd.* He even got Justin once, making him believe that he had been convicted of tax evasion and that they were about to confiscate his home, his cars, everything he owned. It brought him to tears before Ashton let him off the hook and in on the joke.

"Nice try," I said, as I waited for Ashton to come out of hiding.

"What?"

"Tell Ashton, nice try," I said.

Cindy laughed as she promised me that Ashton had nothing to do with this call.

As the truth of what she was telling me began to sink in, I became stunned with disbelief. How could this be? My mind raced back to the times my dad and granddaddy had taken me to watch the launches of the space shuttle and all the dreams I had had as a little boy of going into space. Now that dream might actually come true!

When I was able to breathe again, I told her, "No matter what it takes, let's do what we have to do to make this happen."

"Okay," Cindy said, always the realist in my life, "but you understand this means that everything else you have going for the break will go away."

I told her I did and was willing to take the chance.

All the pieces seemed to fit together perfectly. Very rarely do you get to have any of your big dreams actually come true. I'd already had my pop-star fantasy realized with

*NSYNC; now I was about to have a shot at the other, to be a spaceman.

If everything went right, my plan was to leave for Russia as soon as I could, to begin my cosmonaut training. The timing couldn't have been better. It was the first real break the band had taken in years that afforded us the chance to go out and be on our own. We could finally shift into a different gear and start looking to make lives rather than continue to worry about making livings.

To celebrate the approaching break, I went to a club in Orlando one night. This was one of the few times that my local buddies and I actually had a little time to hit the clubs. Most of the time we'd stay together in one of our homes and just chill. It was late and there was a good feeling happening in the club when this girl came up to me. Her name was Monica. She said she was a fan and wanted to say hi. She was with this guy she introduced as her friend. His name was Jesse. *Wow,* I thought to myself, *now he's good-looking.* I especially liked the way he tried to act all cool, supermacho and aloof. We wound up really clicking.

I liked Monica a lot, but I found myself attracted to Jesse. He told me he was a senior at UCF (University of Central Florida). I wondered in the back of my mind if he wasn't some kind of spoiled rich Miami boy. Anyway, we all got into my car and drove off for some pizza before I took them both back to their places. After, I had to laugh to myself on the way home. I knew Monica thought I was hitting on her, but actually Jesse was the one I was interested in. She lived farther away than Jesse, but I decided to drop her off first. That's when she finally got what was happening.

I went back with Jesse to his place, and before he went in we sat outside in the car just talking for what seemed like hours. I was so happy to have met someone I was actually interested in. And so nervous. Neither one of us knew with any certainty if the other one was gay. Then suddenly he looked at me and said, "I'm going to kiss you right now. Either you can stop me or not." I didn't.

This was the first kiss I'd ever had in my life that made me feel like I was in love.

I managed to see Jesse a couple more times before it was time for me to leave for Russia. He was still into playing cool. I couldn't help myself and started telling all my friends about this great new "girl" I had met. I'm not sure I fooled anyone, especially Beth or Wendy—or really *anybody*—but I wasn't ready to face what I thought would be the heavy consequences of my coming out. Everybody I told seemed happy for me and unchallenging. Believe me, that was a big comfort factor at the time.

I was so crazy about Jesse that I wrote a song for him called "These Eyes." I found inspiration in Jesse that made me want to sit down and try to write songs. I loved him for that as much as everything else. When I sang it for Wendy, she said it was great. Later on she told me she'd known from the very first moment I'd met Jesse that I had been in love with him. Beth even asked me if I was gay during all of this, and I vehemently denied it. I tried to tell her once or twice, but each time we sat down for one of our heart-to-heart boy-girl gal-pal conversations, I chickened out. I just wasn't ready.

When I finally did take off on my space adventure, I had mixed feelings about leaving Jesse behind. I think he did as well. Our last night together we said quick, unemotional good-byes, and in the morning I boarded a plane bound for Moscow.

I hoped he would still be there when I returned.

Chapter Five

The originul concept for the reality show attached to the space mission was that contestants would go through rigorous training and the winner would get a place on a Russian launch aboard the Soyuz. The show part had already been done once, in Denmark, but at the last minute the Danish government would not allow the winner to go to Russia to make the flight. At that point an American producer acquired the rights for a U.S. version and took it to John Ferriter at William Morris to see if a deal could be put together. Ferriter was to serve as the packager of the project, the one to coordinate all the different players and unify the team. Although he didn't actually represent the producer, John put him together with another producer, Phil Gurin, who had been pitching similar types of projects and had the rights to a successful space competition show called *The Big Mission.*

At first the idea was for me to be the host of the show. Very quickly, however, the "game show" concept fell apart, and it was decided that a much better direction to go in would be to do a documentary of me training to become a cosmonaut and actually going up into space. The mission was to take ten days: two days aboard the Soyuz to get to the International Space Station (ISS), which is jointly controlled by the United States and several other nations, then about a week living in space, and at the end I'd leave the space station with my crewmates in a different Soyuz and ultimately land in the desert in Kazakhstan.

The producer hit upon the idea of using me, he said, when he was sitting around with a friend trying to figure out who would be good for the project. The friend's little girl, who was nine years old, blurted out, "Lance Bass wants to go into space!" She knew my lifelong wish from an online chat I had done; one of the questions was "What is your biggest dream?" and I had responded, "To go into space." So everything that followed happened because of a nine-year-old girl who was a fan of mine.

I'd already been concerned that for the past several years the space program had been going down in the public eye, that it had become stale and uninteresting to a lot of young people especially. I hoped my participation might get them excited about it again.

When my mother first heard about the plan, she called me up and asked, quite calmly, if anything in my childhood had happened to make me such a risk-taker and lover of danger. I chuckled and said, "Mom, maybe it's because I had such a good childhood that I'm able to do the things I really like to do."

I didn't have to think about it at all. As soon as the opportunity became real, I went for it. I wanted to be the youngest person to ever go into space, a "space tourist," and the subject of a feature documentary that would help defray the purported $20 million the Russians wanted for the rights to the seat. The Russians have a central government space agency, which provides some funding for their space program. However, the money allocated is minimal, so they are always looking for private funding sources, and "space tourism" is a big component.

There had already been two earlier, privately financed space tourists: an American businessman, Dennis Tito, and a gentleman from South Africa named Mark Shuttleworth, whom I am now happy to call a friend. Mark was just leaving Star City, Russia, when I arrived for training, and he proved to be a great mentor. He also gave me the name of Christine Chiodo, who works in the Space Flight Training Division of NASA and is involved in coordinating the training pieces of the American space program with its international partners, primarily the Russians.

I had all the right preliminary qualifications: I was young, I was in a very popular music group (so the program would get a lot of attention), and I was an avid fan of all things related to space. As my first big dream had been to be an astronaut, it seemed to me a total no-brainer—the perfect project while the band was off the road and out of the studio.

A camera crew followed me to Russia, intending to film virtually every step, from the training to the actual Soyuz journey to the International Space Station to my triumphant return home to Earth. Meanwhile, word began to leak out about the possibility of the upcoming mission. Fans began holding up signs at our last shows that said things like LANCE, WE ARE OVER THE MOON FOR YOU, SHOOT FOR THE MOON, and GO FOR IT. On websites I was referred to as "Lance Basstronaut." I loved it!

However, the whole thing almost ended before it began when the Russians informed us that there was no way I could be properly trained in six months. They insisted it would take almost a year, which was six months more than I had. They wanted me on a March 2003 space flight, but I had to be back in the studio with *NSYNC by December 2002. It was February 2002 when we were having these discussions. The band's hiatus would begin in May, and my training was originally set to begin immediately after the tour, for an October flight. Just when it looked like everything had come apart, the Russians made an about-face and okayed the October mission by condensing my training schedule to four months if I agreed to double up on studies during the day and train most weekends.

The next major obstacle to emerge was my health. Every potential cosmonaut must go through a series of rigorous health tests, and as I quickly learned, there are only two grades: pass or fail. In order to pass you have to be in perfect physical and mental health. The usual requirements for preflight medical testing take two weeks. Due to my touring schedule I had to make two separate trips to Russia to get all of mine done. I would have a few days between *NSYNC dates, and we would fly to Russia for testing at the IBMP (Institute for Biomedical

Problems). On one visit I had literally only a few hours between getting off a fifteen-hour flight from Russia and jumping on stage for a show.

During the testing I received an obligatory colonoscopy. Fine, except I had no idea I was going to be getting one! They gave me no sedation, nothing. They just had me bend over and shoved a magnesium flashlight up my butt. It was so painful I had tears coming down my face. *And then they started laughing at me!* I asked my translator why they were laughing, and he said, "Well, we know now for certain you are not gay!"

I may have been a "regular guy" to them, but nevertheless I'd always had an irregular heartbeat. I'd first become aware of it two years earlier, just as the *No Strings Attached* tour was coming to an end. During one of the final shows I got terribly sick with what I thought was a stomach virus. I'd never felt so bad before in my life. Of course, on tour no matter how bad you feel you have to go on for the sake of the others.

Our tours always ended back home in Florida. I got so sick during those final shows, suffering from dehydration, with lips as chapped as the surface of the moon, that my mom took me directly to the sports medicine clinic to get some fluids and to make sure there was nothing seriously wrong with me. They immediately admitted me for dehydration and put an IV in me. As a result I had to miss two shows of the tour—Tampa and Fort Lauderdale—a first in all the years of being with the band. Fortunately, the rest of the guys were able to go on and have fun winging it. At one point they even brought out one of my bodyguards to take my place onstage. Still, there were a lot of things that couldn't be done if I wasn't there, because of the nature of the choreography.

It was while I was in the hospital that the doctors first noticed something irregular about my heartbeat. They decided to run a few tests and found that it was nothing more serious than an arrhythmia, or irregular heartbeat, something that I had possibly lived with for my whole life. There were no overt symptoms except slight lethargy—that was maybe the reason I liked to sleep so much, but it never interfered with my ability to do a show. Funny enough, whenever I was exerting myself, like when I was performing, my heart always beat normally. It was only while resting that the irregular rhythm would occur.

Sure enough, it showed up again at one of my pre–space training physicals in Russia, and the doctors there told me I would not be able to go into space unless it was corrected. They gave me a month to get it fixed or all bets were off.

That freaked me out, but I knew I had to have it done if I wanted to be a cosmonaut. And because I was under all kinds of deadline constraints, I couldn't take a lot of time to make a decision. My parents were a bit frightened at the thought of the procedure. My dad spoke with a number of cardiologists and was determined to find the best in the country. On May 1, 2002, my mom and dad, Cindy, and Wendy arrived with me at Beth Israel Deaconess Hospital in Boston. Dr. Mark Josephson, one of the best cardiac surgeons in the world, was scheduled to perform a corrective heart ablation on me. Dr. Josephson assured me there was nothing to worry about. I have to tell you, though, at first I was more worried about the doctor than I was about the surgery. Dr. Josephson was a fun doctor. He'd show up wearing a sheriff's badge, for instance. I suppose he was trying to put me at ease. But he was dead serious about the surgery. He said it was not customary to do this type of operation on a person with a totally benign condition. The normal treatment is to do nothing, and Dr. Josephson had strongly advised me to think twice before going ahead. He was right about the fact that no operation is ever a good thing to have, especially elective surgery.

However, I knew I wasn't going to be able to go into space with an irregular heartbeat, so there was no other

choice: I told him to go ahead. Because the entire space
adventure was being filmed for the documentary, there
were cameras recording every moment, including the
operation. I remember everything that happened quite
clearly because I was awake for the entire procedure.
It took several hours, and there were television screens
everywhere, so I could see exactly what they were doing.
They sent catheters through my arteries from my groin
and kept on pumping me full of adrenaline so my heart
would beat faster and they could pinpoint the problems.
It was eerie; I could feel the wires traveling up inside me,
and I had this vaguely metallic taste in my mouth. I had
a button to push for the anesthesiologist, and when it
really hurt she'd increase the morphine drip. I remember they played music throughout the entire procedure.
Dr. Josephson preferred Aretha Franklin because, he said,
she kept him in a good mood. Once he found the right
spot, he sent microwaves through me to mark the piece
they wanted, and believe me, I pushed that morphine
button so fast I almost broke it off the machine!

Later on, after it was all over, Dr. Josephson told me
that he did find something else that was wrong, which he
corrected during the procedure; it was no serious problem then, but if left unchecked it could have been far

more serious later on in my life. At that moment I felt extremely lucky. The good news is that my heartbeat has been perfectly regular ever since.

To help facilitate my training and make sure that everything stayed on schedule, Cindy agreed to come along to Russia with me for the first three weeks, until I got settled in and everything was running smoothly.

I trained in Star City, Russia, about an hour and a half outside of Moscow, at the Yuri Gagarin Cosmonaut Training Center, named for the first man ever to go up into space. Cindy and I lived in a *prophy*, something resembling a college dormitory, only not nearly as nice. It was at the height of the legendary Russian summer heat and humidity when we first arrived. And of course the *prophy* had no air-conditioning. I eventually put one in, and every hour all through the night I'd have to wake up and empty the cup where the condensation had collected.

Back in the day Gagarin Cosmonaut Training Center (GCTC) was a secret training facility. It was established in the early 1960s, and the community in general still sort of has that nostalgic feel to it. The people who live in Star City are for the most part GCTC workers or GCTC

workers' families. It's a little village in the middle of the
forest where everyone seems to know everyone else. Inside
this walled community is another, smaller walled village,
and that is where all the cosmonaut training takes place.
No one was allowed back there except for the cosmonauts
and their trainers.

One of the first things I did upon returning to Star
City and beginning my formal training was to get fitted
for my space suit and other necessary space gear. That put
me on a complete high, even if the experience itself wasn't
so great. Every astronaut and cosmonaut who travels in
the Soyuz has to have a special seat liner custom-made for
them. Having mine made was a trip! I was basically given
long underwear to put on and then had to lie on my back
with my knees up to my chest in sort of a cross between
a bathtub and a coffin while people poured wet plaster
over me up to my neck. The tricky part is that it has to be
made so that when you're in space and your body grows
(which it does a little bit because there's no gravity), the
suit will accommodate you.

As it turned out, the main stumbling block was one
that would plague us throughout the entire time we were
in Russia: money. To let you in on what we were dealing with in terms of people's hunger for money—Cindy

needed a computer line in her *prophy* room. The Russians wanted twenty-five hundred dollars to install it plus a thousand dollars a month. Still, we tried to keep a positive attitude the entire four months we were in Russia. No matter what, I was determined to keep my cool, keep smiling, and stay happy. It had been no easy task to get this far, and I was aware that despite having jumped what felt like a million hurdles I still had a million more to go.

All throughout training my team tried to keep the financial end afloat. Normally, on a project like this, rule number one is that you have all the financing in place before anything else. However, because we had to rush everything in order for me to make the October flight, we had to go about this backward and hope for the best. It was a chance I was willing to take.

My team explained to me that we were walking into this with nothing completely secure. We had a contract with a major network that was in negotiations, close but not yet signed, and we had only a letter of intent from a major sponsor—a popular breakfast drink for $10 million for their brand to be on my spacesuit. There was other sponsor interest that looked great, especially if we were formally attached to a major network. Due to the deadline constraints and my limited time off from the band, I had to make a decision, so I decided to shoot for the moon. I wanted this so bad that I was willing to move forward on spec although nothing was for sure. What's that old saying? "You miss 100 percent of the chances you never take."

The Russians had no intention of letting anyone get away with what might even appear to the most casual observer as a free ride. From the beginning they demanded $20 million before I would be able to complete my training.

At first the training was really fun, although I was aware from the very beginning that I was under extraordinary scrutiny. One time when I was away for the weekend I wasn't aware that the gate closed in the middle of Star City and that there was an open gate on the other side of the woods. So I simply scaled the wall to get to my gym class. The next week I was a little late, but now I knew how to get in. Because I had to go around to the other side, I was late, and the first thing the instructor asked me was why I didn't scale the wall the way I had the last time. That gave me chills. They knew every move I made.

There was a tremendous amount of heavy, intense physical training, including centrifuge. Centrifuge is a machine that spins around and manipulates the force of gravity. The purpose is to simulate the amount of force during descent, when the Soyuz returns to Earth. They strap you into a chair and spin you around to test your endurance. At one point I think I got up to five g's, which felt like seven hundred fifty pounds pressing on my chest, which is very intense!

There is also survival and emergency training, where they take you out to the woods and you learn how to build shelters, start fires, and find food, and you do it for hours and hours. It's usually done with the rest of your crew, but since mine had already been through it, I had to do it by myself. It was difficult and lonely, but at least I got to do it in the summer. The cosmonauts who fly in April have to do it in the winter, spending three nights all alone surviving by themselves. The Russian winter is not a pleasant experience.

A lot of the training for my mission was learning to survive in entirely different environments than normal. I had to relearn how to live: how to eat, how to make food, how to drink, how to move around, even how to go to the bathroom while I was in space. For example, the Soyuz capsule seats three people, and it's the most uncomfortable ride imaginable. My knees were forced up into my chest sometimes for hours. It was horribly cramped with two other guys right next to me at all times in a space about the size of the backseat of a Volkswagen Beetle. Sometimes these sessions lasted four hours, because it takes two days to reach the space station, and endurance is a big part of the training.

Shortly after our arrival in Russia they took Cindy and me to see the actual Soyuz capsule. For months she had been dealing with this project and it was only talk and papers. When she finally saw the capsule that I would be squeezed into for two days, traveling at a speed of 17,900 miles an hour, the reality of it hit her for the first time. She said to me, "You know, Lance, it is not too late to pull out. You don't have to do this." I appreciated her concerns, but I wasn't about to back out. This was my dream, and I was so close now I could taste it!

Now I was training in the Soyuz, plus I was trying to cram-learn all this theory and practical, hands-on rocket science. Everyone who goes up has to know every nut and bolt of the craft, every molecular equation, and all emergency procedures: What to do if a meteor hits the space station or the Soyuz, what if a fire breaks out—every possible contingency. As I quickly discovered, the Russians don't make much of a distinction between a space tourist and someone who is actually part of the cosmonaut program. In truth, if there actually had been an emergency aboard, there was probably no way in the world they would have relied on me other than to make sure I didn't touch anything, but the training didn't reflect that. I was made to feel that I could handle any type of emergency that arose.

All of it was doubly difficult for me because, unlike professional astronauts and cosmonauts, I had no prior technical background in things like orbital mechanics, nor did I get much time training with my actual flight crew. Now I was about to take up a brand-new Soyuz and had to learn everything about it—and in Russian. The interpreters they had were probably earning about ten dollars a week, and as a result there was a lot of turnover (especially of the good ones), so much of the time I was working with interpreters who were really inexperienced. It was another strike against me, because I already had to condense the training program due to the time constraints of *NSYNC's hiatus.

As Christine Chiodo later put it, absorbing all of this in such a short time was like trying to drink from a fire hose. One of the biggest compliments she paid me was how impressed she was that I learned as much as I did.

* * *

There were two different rocket systems involved on this particular mission, one to take it up and one to bring it back. To master them, I took a daily intensive-study class to understand enough of the Russian language to at least know what they were talking about when they were trying to teach me.

They had me in Russian classes every day for four hours a day without a break. I had this teacher, Igor, who only spoke Russian and French. He would come to my room at the *prophy*, we'd sit at the breakfast table, and we would stare at each other for four hours, trying to learn words. I'd know how to conjugate everything but have no idea what it meant. Eventually I picked up enough to get around, but not strictly from Igor. Sometimes it felt like every word I learned came from people we met from NASA who were living in Russia at the time, Russians who spoke English, taking taxicabs, and just being in the country for so long.

Cindy always says I have the attention span of a gnat (which is true). That's why she was so amazed in the evening when she would ask me study questions for my tests and I could answer every one with ease. My first exam was the hardest: all rocket science. A lot was riding on this one, because if I failed, it would mean that I wasn't capable of learning what I needed to know to go up in space. It was a verbal test, with NASA and Russian representatives present in the room. I got a five, the highest score possible. I guess it goes to show that you can learn the most difficult things when you are interested in them.

I had some experiments planned for space. I was going to do environmental studies of the Mississippi Delta involving a lot of photography, and assist the others with experiments in blood studies. And for the younger generation I wanted to create videos, all to stimulate and renew scholastic interest in the space program.

Due to the language barrier I thought the taking of my first official photo was a photography *class*. It was six in the morning, and I looked like crap for what turned out to be my official crew portrait. What's really funny is that they put together three of us who'd been training individually up until now, and then they made me get out so they could get some shots of just my two crewmates in case I wasn't there at the end.

Once we met, I got to know my space partners extremely well. I trained with them every day and eventually got into their psyche. I had to, because I had to have their back. Things can go wrong in a split second in space, and I had to be prepared for anything. I even wound up holding the bathroom facilities for them, catching their urine in a gravity-free environment. You quickly become like family.

In my crew the pilot's name was Sergei Zalyotin. The engineer was Belgian, Frank de Winne. Sergei had gone up a couple of times before, and he was this very macho Russian cosmonaut type, a real ladies' man. And he didn't speak a lick of English. Early on I sensed that he didn't care at all if I was going along on the mission or not. Frank, on the other hand, was a brilliant rocket scientist who spoke great English and I got the feeling he was totally against my being on board. He made Sergei seem in comparison like my mother. This was Frank's first spaceflight, and he may have felt that sharing it with a pop star degraded his accomplishment.

Back at the *prophy*, Cindy and I were literally living off Pringles, peanut butter, Snickers, and macaroni and cheese because we were not particularly fond of the Russian "cuisine" that was available at Star City. Our diet there was so bad that I couldn't wait to go into Moscow on the rare weekends I had time off and eat at McDonald's. Those golden arches never looked so good!

I also had to attend psychiatric evaluations once a week to make sure I was going to be mentally capable of dealing with all the stresses of space flight. Part of the training included being familiarized with all the people I was going to meet up at the space station. They predicted the ones I would get along with in space and the ones I wouldn't. As it happened, the one they said I wouldn't get along with, Ed Lu, was an American astronaut I actually knew and had become friends with. Later on, Ed, who was in space for his own mission, happened to find my space suit waiting at the International Space Station, so he ripped my name tag off the front, floated the tag in space with Earth behind it, and took a picture of it for me. I appreciated the gesture!

Because *NSYNC had never played Russia, I was able to walk the streets and not be recognized, which, while a great relief to me, also felt a little odd. We had been so big for so long that the need for bodyguards had become second nature whenever we went out in most public places. Gradually, as word got out that I was training for the flight, I did sense a difference; the Russian people began to recognize me as a cosmonaut-in-training and wanted my autograph when they would see me out and about in Moscow.

But it was nothing like what was going on back in the States. My publicist, Jill Fritzo, was being besieged with questions and requests about my upcoming scheduled launch. We never knew how people got the number, but Cindy kept receiving calls on her Russian cell phone from major network news anchors who wanted the first sit-down interview after I returned from space. We were getting six-figure offers for me to come speak at colleges about my flight experience. It was crazy, and I hadn't even flown yet.

Meanwhile, our days in Russia were long and difficult. The sun rose at seven and didn't set until eleven, and the mosquitoes were always out and hungry for our blood. I counted dozens of bites on my arms and legs each morning when I woke up. And sometimes we had no hot water. I didn't mind roughing it the way we did, but poor Cindy, the type who likes to iron her sweatpants, was having a much tougher time. Here she had been my manager for less than six months and she was living in Russia with me. It had become clear that she was going to have to be there full-time to run interference for all the roadblocks coming our way with the deal. Also, I know she didn't want to leave me there all by myself. I told her I was going to name my first daughter after her for all she had been through. She said I was going to have to do a heck of a lot more than that.

Our nighttime in Russia was daytime in the States, so she was literally on the phone around the clock. My agent and my attorney in the States had conference calls scheduled with her almost nightly, with their alarm clocks set for the wee hours of the morning. Everyone was so incredibly dedicated and hell-bent on making this happen.

Cindy and I became very close to some of the NASA people and their families who lived in the cottages just across the way from the *prophy*. They proved a saving grace for us and a little piece of the home that we so desperately missed. We'd go down late in the evening and hang out with the other astronauts in Shep's Bar. Bill Shepherd was the first commander of the ISS. When the crew's cottages in Star City were being built, he always said that what they (the Star City Americans) really needed was a place for everyone to go relax and hang out together. He thought they should turn the basement of one of the cottages into a bar. So, as a surprise to him, while he was back in the United States training for a few months, some NASA personnel got together and turned the basement of his cottage into Shep's Bar.

They were all anxious to surprise Shep upon his return to Star City, and then they got really lucky: Tom Hanks (a big space fan as well) just happened to be in Russia, and they were able to get him to come to the opening. When Shep arrived back in Star City, they told him they had a surprise for him and sent him downstairs to the basement of his cottage. He found that not only had his basement been transformed into a bar, but Tom Hanks was standing behind the counter playing bartender. How cool!

It was an honor to be surrounded by NASA astronauts and people who shared the same passion that I had. We'd stay down there for hours shooting pool, listening to the jukebox, reminiscing about home, and talking about my flight. The jukebox had about a hundred songs in it, and they quickly got old. Funny enough, *NSYNC was a part of the selection.

In the middle of my training in Russia, Cindy and I, along with my crewmates, went to Houston, Texas, to train at Johnson Space Center for a week. NASA asks all space tourists to do that. There was a familiar face waiting for us there: Christine Chiodo.

We were just so grateful to be back on American soil. Our families met us over there. We had never been so glad to see their faces in all our lives. Being surrounded by Americans made all the difference to me. I remember thinking to myself how much easier everything would have been if I could have done all my training in America, in English, right from the start! NASA is not a big fan of what they consider "amateur" space tourism or the fact that seats can be bought on Russian flights by virtually anyone with enough money. It's one of the reasons NASA wants to train the space tourists themselves for a week, to try and prepare them for any emergency that might happen up at the space station itself. I felt that now that NASA knew how committed I was, they embraced me. They even asked me to do some lecturing to students, which I was thrilled to do.

By the time my training ended, I felt I was as prepared as I was ever going to be. When I had my final certification exam, I faced a panel of about eight Russians I had never seen before. They asked me questions about the Soyuz in Russian, which—along with my answers—had to be translated to complete the evaluation.

Finally, on July 2, 2002, I was named as an official candidate to be a space tourist on the scheduled October Soyuz flight. The news quickly spun through the media all over the world. Now we had a definite launch date for October. The launch itself was set for Kazakhstan, because of its favorable location closer to the equator, in the absolute middle of nowhere. Because of the necessary three-day quarantine prior to the actual liftoff, my family would have to visit with me through a glass window prior to the launch.

A launch that never happened.

With the Russians, it was all about the contract. The $20 million was their primary focus, and they were determined to collect all of it before I went up twenty feet. It was to be divided among three factions: the Yuri Gagarin Cosmonaut Training Center, the RSA (Russian Space Agency—the Russian government agency equivalent to NASA), and Energia, the Russian contractor who actually builds the spacecraft and operates the Russian equivalent of Houston's Mission Control. Gagarin and Energia operate essentially as private businesses. Anyway, the first payment had been made by our producer via one of our potential sponsors, but the other part, the network's share, had not come through. They were stalling, and we had no idea why.

As our problems continued to mount, word somehow began leaking out to the press back in the States that the flight was in trouble. My team and I had to sign extensive nondisclosure agreements and were unable to discuss any-thing in the press. It was hard for us to not respond to the negative untruths that were making headlines, but that would have for sure gotten me thrown out of the program and probably the country.

So many things happened next that were beyond our control. My publicist, Jill, arranged for a major national publication to have the exclusive first shot of me in my spacesuit for its cover. We were boiling mad when a photo was leaked out of Russia and ended up in the news section of a rag magazine. Senseless things like this continued to happen. There were times we felt completely helpless. I'd read on more than one occasion that my attempt to go into space was nothing more than a publicity stunt. The whole idea that this could possibly be a hoax would have been hilarious if it hadn't been so unfunny. For one thing, from all the gravity training and my elective surgery my height and weight had dramatically changed by the time I came home. Does that sound like a joke?

It killed us when my business team learned that the major network that we were in negotiations with was not prepared to move forward with me. They appear to have used me in Russia like a guinea pig. They wanted the Soyuz seat for a game show they were hoping to air. The scrambling then began back in Hollywood to try to get new funding from other sources. As the window of my opportunity to go up in space continued to narrow, John Ferriter desperately tried to cobble together a last-minute deal with MTV and another one with the Discovery Channel. We did manage to get a number of sponsor commitments from a toothpaste company, a hair-care product, and a soft drink. We even had the advertisements approved for one sponsor with me holding the product.

However, MTV finally backed out over payment, insurance, and indemnification issues that were simply unsolvable. They didn't want to make the rest of their payment until I was successfully launched, and the Russians wouldn't let me go into space until the rest of the money was paid. MTV was understandably concerned that the Russians could pull out of the deal at the last possible minute without financial penalties. In other words MTV wanted their investment insured against the Russians changing their minds. Everything else possible was covered by a Lloyd's of London policy, but even they wouldn't insure against the possibility of Russian capriciousness.

We had one sponsor that had committed to advertising on the capsule, but they too pulled out at the last minute. They said they were worried about what would happen if I was killed in space—not worried about me, mind you, but about their image and the sales of their products and what my death might do to their brand.

To the Russians, though, our end of it was all immaterial. They didn't want to know our problems; all they wanted was their money, and since I had the contract with them I was the one they insisted had to pay. More than once I got kicked out of Star City in the middle of training over some money dispute, and I'd have to stay in a hotel in Moscow, missing precious days sitting around until somebody bailed me out.

Cindy, John, and Adam were all now frantically manning the phones trying to hold the deal together, hoping to keep the business weight off my shoulders so I could be free to concentrate on my training. I was again pulled out of class by the Russians wanting to talk about when they would receive the balance of their money. We knew it was all imploding, but I hadn't come this far not to be a certified cosmonaut, so I agreed to personally fund the rest of the training—regardless of whether or not there would be a TV show, or even if the launch took place—for what amounted to about four hundred fifty thousand dollars out of my own pocket. After that, I finished the training with no further interruptions, got my certificate, and was ready to go into space.

Still, though I had come so close to going into space, gained my official certification, and gone through the craziest four months of my life, the sad truth is that I never even got to see the launchpad. My trip was finally and irrevocably canceled by the Russians over, unsurprisingly, money. We still might have been able to pull it off if I had been able to sign on for the March 2003 launch. That would have given us more time, but it was out of the question. My time off from the band had run out. The six-month break we had agreed to was over, and I was due back in the studio to start work on the next *NSYNC album.

So much effort by so many people had gone up in smoke. What really hurt was that we had gone through so much and actually gotten *so close*. It was heartbreaking; there is no other word for it.

Despite being in what amounted to a state of emotional exhaustion, I managed to get to Orlando. The first thing my friends noticed was how much smaller I was and that my skin looked ashen. It was, I told them, from the lack of any direct exposure to sunlight and the rigorous training schedule. They said I looked thinner. I had lost thirty pounds during this ordeal.

Even the green in my eyes had faded.

I have to say that my parents and all my friends were relieved that for whatever reason I wasn't going through with the mission. My mom, especially, had been scared to death the whole time. I could understand how everyone close to me felt, but it was also extremely embarrassing for me when the whole thing fizzled out like it did. I felt that I had been living a lot of dreams, for myself, for my fans, and for my friends, and that somehow I had let them all down. It was hard to deal with and keep upbeat. I had gone in with a smile and had wanted to come out smiling. I made up my mind to keep my head up and try to look happy even if inside I was hurt really bad.

I tried to find some positives in all that had gone down. I became the Youth Spokesperson for World Space Week. I still travel and speak to students to encourage them to stay in school and study math and science if they are interested in one day having a career in aeronautics. Great things like that came out of my experience.

However bad I felt, I had no time to feel sorry for myself. I had to gear myself up to return to being a member of the most popular band in the world. It was like

changing into my secret identity as a mild-mannered bass
singer. The more I got my head on straight about it, the
happier I really became, unaware that I was about to face
two different and far more devastating losses than a seat
on a spaceship. One had to do with the exposure of my
private sexuality to the whole world, and the other was
the unexpected, shattering breakup of *NSYNC.

To tell you the truth, I don't know which one was
worse.

Chapter Six

To me *NSYNC was like family, and family, as I know it, stays together.

Being like brothers, we ate together, slept together, traveled together, performed together, lived together, and fought with one another. At the end of the day, no matter what went down, we were still like blood. I loved that and because of it believed *NSYNC would stay together forever.

In May 2002 *NSYNC took the stage at T. D. Waterhouse Arena in Orlando for the final show of our tour, after which the band had agreed to take a six-month hiatus. The house was packed, overflowing with fans. All of our parents were there, and the feeling in the place was electric. We were at the peak of our careers, the top of our game, and yet there was something weird in the air that I couldn't pinpoint. I didn't know it then, but this was to be the very last time ever we would perform live before a concert audience as *NSYNC.

Usually, at the end of a tour everyone, right down to the last stagehand, is excited and happy, exhilarated by all that has been accomplished. But, like the rest of the band, that night I felt physically exhausted, weak, and more than ready for a little break from the others and the constant traveling and performing, which had all but consumed every last ounce of my strength. All of us had agreed that after nearly seven years of recording, promotion, and touring, the chance to take a real break from *NSYNC was not just something we'd welcome but was long overdue.

Each of us in the band—Joey, Chris, JC, Justin, and I—looked forward to doing things as individuals during the break, separate and apart from being members of *NSYNC. We all had private lives that we wanted to pursue, our own friends outside of the band, and projects to develop. I had to agree with the others that a little "summer vacation" was just what the doctor ordered. A limited absence would, I believed, make all of our hearts grow a little fonder toward the band of brothers we called *NSYNC.

The idea of taking a sabbatical had first come to light the previous December, traditionally one of the slowest months for touring. We were in Orlando, and in between dates we taped a song for an MTV Christmas special for an audience of fan-contest winners, where they got a chance to exchange gifts with us (for our charity) at a hotel near Disney World.

The large hotel suite we were filming in was decorated for Christmas, with trees and wreaths and lights strung. We were dressed in Christmas sweaters for the sake of filming, even though it was typically warm Florida weather. Everyone seemed to be having a great time and yet, despite the joyful atmosphere, it didn't seem like a very festive occasion to us. Holiday or no holiday, we were as usual working our butts off. On this particular day MTV had arranged for fans to come in and meet us after the show, something we always enjoyed doing but that usually left us all exhausted by the time the last hand was shaken, the last photo smiled for, the last autograph signed.

After, we all went back to our rooms. Joey and I were stretched out on the bed listening to CDs when Justin came in and said that he needed to talk to us about something. "When this tour ends, I'd like for us to take a six-month break. I'm thinking about fooling around with a solo album. Jive wants me to do it. I don't know if I'll even finish it or if it'll ever be released."

My first reaction was, *Cool!* I was always in favor of individual projects for every one of us. I believed that anything successful that one member did outside the band only made the group as a whole that much stronger.

Joey and I agreed that a break that long would be a good thing. Justin sighed as if in relief and sat back in his chair, looking much more relaxed than when he'd come in. "Hey, guys, I doubt if it'll even get released," he repeated, as if to ease our minds. "It's just something I want to work on. It'll probably take years to get it right!" With that he smiled, got up, and left.

JC came in next, and we could tell he was upset. "Well," he said, "I think it's great for Justin but may be the beginning of the end."

"Oh, come on," I said. "Justin's not going to break up the group. We're fine."

And that's what I said and that's what I believed.

After all, we had taken breaks before without incident, although not for this long. A year earlier, in the summer of 2001, prior to the recording of the *Celebrity* album and the PopOdyssey tour, the group had decided to take three months off. During that time Joey and I had made a movie together up in Canada called *On the Line*. And a year before then, Justin had made a movie as well, a TV film for Disney called *Model Behavior*, and JC had produced a couple of recordings with the outside groups Boyz-N-Girls United and (all-girl group) Wild Orchid. So, despite JC's fear, this latest request for a hiatus seemed fine to me.

It wasn't that Joey and I were looking for careers as movie actors away from the band. In truth Joey and I had made *On the Line* only after serious talks had taken place with Tom Hanks's production company about the possibility of making an *NSYNC feature film. I loved the idea from the beginning. I'd seen those old Beatles movies: *A Hard Day's Night, Help!, Yellow Submarine*, and *Let It Be*. The early ones, especially, were so funny and goofy they looked like they must have been a blast to make. The Beatles reminded us of ourselves, and I thought it would be great if our fans could see that side of us on film. Not only that, but the Beatles' popularity and record sales soared every time one of their films came out. And you can imagine the soundtrack! That was the kind of creative enterprise I wanted to do with *NSYNC, but for one reason or another the rest of the guys in the band weren't that into it. When I finally realized it wasn't going to happen, at least not that summer, I put the deal together with Miramax for *On the Line* starring Joey and me.

It was a low-budget project and totally fun to make. However, halfway through it Joey and I got word from the rest of the group that they wanted to get back into the studio as soon as possible. That could have caused a bit of a problem, because we were shooting the film in Toronto. The last thing we wanted to do was split our concentration between the movie and a new album. But our first priority was always *NSYNC, so we worked out a schedule that allowed us to continue shooting in Toronto during the week and fly down to Orlando on weekends to work with the band.

Predictably, things got a little crazy for Joey and me. One day we were shooting in Canada and the next we were flying down to Florida to lay down tracks for the upcoming *Celebrity* album, learning the steps for the upcoming PopOdyssey tour, and doing cover shoots for all the major magazines that were writing about the band.

I had dyed my hair brown for the movie, and now every time I went to Florida to be with *NSYNC to take promotional photos I had to bleach it back to blond. This went on until my hair started falling out and what I had left turned a bottom-of-the-ocean greenish brown. As a result I had to have hair extensions put on my head just to look like me! (If you look closely at the movie, you can see my hair turn various shades of brown.)

One time during the shooting of the film, Justin flew up to Toronto to visit, and while he was there we recorded some tracks together. That was the first time I ever heard "Gone." We went off in his car and he played me a rough mix of "Gone," which he'd just written for the band. I immediately thought to myself that it was going to be a huge hit.

As soon as our film was complete, both Joey and I went full tilt into *NSYNC mode.

During the PopOdyssey tour, Joey and I didn't have time to promote the film. Instead we had the actual trailer play in the stadiums before our concerts. Still, everything seemed perfect. *NSYNC's album was huge, every date on the tour was completely sold out, we scored a bit at the MTV Awards, and we performed our final show of the tour down in the Bahamas. The premiere of our film was all set for the third week in September . . . and then 9/11 happened.

That was not only the effective end of our upcoming promotional campaign for the film, but of the film itself. In light of the national tragedy our movie couldn't mean a hill of beans to anyone, including us. There was nothing we could have done to change that fact. Our film was finished and we knew it, but we went ahead anyway and did the one press junket that had already been set up, where we sat in our hotel room and were interviewed by reporter after reporter. At one point we found ourselves in the same hotel with Drew Barrymore, who was promoting her own movie one floor below, and Jimmy Woods promoting his one floor above. However, the pallor in the air was unavoidable.

Halfway through the press junket, the president declared war and that was it—our film was finished. We had wanted to entertain America, to give back some good feelings, but once the country went to war, there was no way our film was going to be on anyone's top-priority list.

When the six-month hiatus ended, we all expected to begin work right away on a new album. It fell to our manager, Johnny Wright, to inform the rest of us that Justin felt he needed more time to work on his solo album and didn't know how long it was going to take. Suddenly, I had more time on my hands than I knew what to do with.

In 2002 *NSYNC performed for the 2002 Winter Olympics festivities, and I had the distinct honor of being asked to run with the Olympic torch. This was one of the coolest things I'd ever done. I carried the flame in Newport Beach and was thrilled to meet some of the Olympians in person.

Each runner was to carry the torch a quarter mile. I was the last runner on this leg of the trail and was to stop in front of a boot store where the media was gathered and I would light the caldron. The flame weighed approximately eight pounds, including fuel. Jogging along holding the flame high in one hand and waving to the crowd was exciting. But the flame was getting very heavy, and my arm was shaking. I was glad to see the boot place coming into view. But the truck in front of us carrying the media continued to drive and drive. The boot store came and went. I had no clue what was going on, but I ended up running more than a mile holding eight pounds up in the air. The driver explained that there were a lot of people lined up down the street and he wanted to make sure everyone got to see the flame.

Coming off the high of that, however, came the low of more *NSYNC delays as word came down that the band had to wait yet another six months.

And then another.

Early in 2003 Johnny Wright informed the rest of the band that Justin still needed more time to work on his solo album and that it was going to be at least another six months before *NSYNC could even begin to think about starting the next album.

I was getting a little confused now. It had been almost a year since we'd been in the studio, and I strongly felt the band needed to get back to work. I wasn't the only one in the band growing increasingly impatient, and not without good reason. Cold reality was looking Joey, JC, Chris, and me straight in the face. Without a new album the heat would surely start to leave *NSYNC. In pop music the hard fact of life is and always has been: out of sight, out of mind.

Finally, that fall we were asked to submit fifteen new songs by Christmas as a way of kicking off discussions about the musical direction of the band.

Then, the week before Thanksgiving, we all received word that nothing more was going to happen with the band for at least another year. *Oh, great,* I thought to myself. I had kept my calendar clear from January through September 2004 to make sure nothing conflicted with the making of the band's new CD and the subsequent tour. There were so many things I'd had to turn down, including trying for a later launch date on the Soyuz mission. Now I had nothing concrete to look forward to. All the momentum that we'd worked so hard to build with *NSYNC was gone.

All this downtime translated into lost time. Talk shows, films, all kinds of opportunities had gone by the wayside while I'd waited for the band to come back together. A time when the *NSYNC momentum for us individually was still at its peak.

I'd also spent time trying to write my own songs, hoping that at least one of them might get on the new album. It was the first time I'd ever felt good about writing.

In the summer of 2004, two years after our initial six-month hiatus, the band got back together in Orlando—not to play, but to make an appearance at a celebrity basketball game to raise money for *NSYNC's official charity, Challenge for the Children. The event was a great success. Our roster of guest stars included Queen

Latifah, Destiny's Child, Brian McKnight, Britney Spears, and Eddie George. As we did every year, *NSYNC sang "The Star-Spangled Banner" before the game was played. Although I didn't know it at the time, this performance of our national anthem, which happened to also be the very first song we had sung together, was the last time we would ever perform as *NSYNC.

After the game and festivities we decided to hold our annual *NSYNC meeting to discuss the ongoing business and direction of the band. It was at that meeting that Justin dropped his version of the atomic bomb. He told us what was really happening: that he was trying to find his own sound and was just not feeling the band anymore. He concluded by saying he didn't think it was going to happen because we weren't the same group anymore. His meaning was clear. He went on to talk some more about the group's focus, that he didn't think any of us was operating in the best interests of the band. I asked him what he meant by that, and he said, "Well, you know, when y'all did your movie," meaning Joey and me.

I couldn't believe it. That sounded like the lamest excuse imaginable. Joey and I looked at each other in amazement—like, *whooaaa!* According to Justin, the whole reason for the breakup of *NSYNC was *everyone* *else's* fault? That was crazy! All of us had done nothing but wait around for him to feel he was ready to start work on a new *NSYNC album. What shocked Joey and me especially was that the others quickly seemed to fall in behind Justin, as if they somehow agreed with him that it was our fault!

Wow, I thought to myself, *I must have been completely blind.* I'd always thought that, if anything, our movie would bring new fans to our music. And hadn't Justin made a movie the year before we did ours? As much as I hated to admit it, this was just a lot of smoke being blown to cover up the fact that Justin wanted to leave the band.

I tried to remain calm, but inside I was devastated, as it began to sink in that we were finished, that there was never going to be another new *NSYNC album or another tour. That there was no longer even a group called *NSYNC. My whole life had become defined by my being a member of *NSYNC. I was no longer Lance Bass but "Lance of *NSYNC." I was confused about how and why this had happened. Even though all the warning signs may have been there, this wasn't something I had been expecting. I definitely felt hurt, the result of a lot of miscommunication and misunderstandings that no one seemed willing to talk about. And that's what really got to me. The fact that nobody wanted to talk things over told me that it was really the end. That truth penetrated my soul like a razor-sharp blade slicing directly through my heart.

For that matter, I'm still disappointed with all our actions. I feel we should have spoken up earlier and dealt better with what was happening. We all kind of knew what was going on but still let it happen. Once I came back from Russia and Justin wanted three months more, I realize now that I should have asked more questions. But again, I just didn't have the confidence to do that. So I remained passive and allowed what happened to happen. If only we had said, "Look, just tell us the truth," it would have been better for all of us.

I felt completely betrayed. All of us had been strung along to believe that just beyond the horizon (or was it over the rainbow?) we were going to go back into the studio to make a new album, until someone finally had the guts to tell us it wasn't going to happen. It pissed me off that Justin's life got set up perfectly before he came back to the rest of us. And I felt that Johnny Wright, our manager, had a responsibility to let the four of us know what was happening (or really, what wasn't going to be happening) much sooner.

It felt like the security blanket of my career had suddenly been yanked away from me. My future was now unknown, and the unknown frightened me. Singing, especially in a group, was really the only thing I had any real experience in. It was what I did best. I had hobbies, other interests, film for one, but that had never been my main focus. I simply didn't know what I was going to do.

I needed to know why it had become necessary to shut us down. Why couldn't Justin keep the franchise intact while he also did his own thing? As I thought about it, hard as it was for me to face it, the simple truth slowly became clear. Justin's time to become a solo star had arrived. Looking back at the band's last album and video, I could see now that everything seemed to naturally favor Justin. The record company executives had wanted him to sing all the solos and be in the middle of every shot. It became something of a joke among all of us, even him, that the rest of us were slowly being relegated to his backup singers. Sometimes, during photo shoots, we'd kid around with the photographers and move Justin to the side while putting one of us in the middle; they would always quite "diplomatically" move us back in place. It reminded us of the No Doubt video for "Don't Speak," the one where Gwen Stefani is front and center in the video and the band members are all covered up in the back. We'd even begun to sing "Don't Speak" among ourselves as a way of making fun of what we thought at the time was just some goofy and harmless stuff. It had never occurred to us at the time that we were watching Justin begin to make his exit from the band.

We still hadn't gotten the message when we'd recorded "Gone," the fifth cut on what turned out to be our final album of new material, *Celebrity*. It was the first *NSYNC song that Justin took the whole lead on. He also wrote the song. At the time we were like, *Wow, how great!* It didn't occur to any of us what a song called "Gone" might actually mean. Jive released it as the album's third single ("Pop" and "Girlfriend" were the first two). It did really well, and a few months later Justin began recording his first solo album.

I had tears in my eyes as Justin told us the sad news and Joey did as well. Chris and JC didn't get as emotional; looking back, I tend to think that they were more aware of what was coming than Joey and I were, that maybe Justin had talked to them first before telling us. Even so, I knew that Chris had to be feeling *something* inside. After all, he was the one who had started the group.

I remember after the meeting asking JC if he thought

that this really was the end of *NSYNC. His response was encouraging to me. "I'll keep it going it with four guys if I have to," he said.

That sparked me. "I will too," I said.

"That's right. We can all sing. He can leave if he wants to do his own thing, and come back later if he feels like it, but we can do a new *NSYNC album with four guys instead of five."

I was lit up. I thought maybe if we started recording without him he might even decide at the last minute to lay on some vocals and we'd be together again, at least on record. I stayed hopeful until about a month later, when, back in Orlando from L.A. visiting friends, I ran into JC and discovered that since our last conversation he had apparently changed his tune. Chris wasn't into doing it now without Justin, and JC thought it wouldn't work with only the three of us. Now he was thinking that instead of working on a new *NSYNC album he'd go solo himself.

I told him that was cool. He deserved to be creative in his own way as much as Justin did in his.

Looking back, in the immediate aftermath of the band's breakup I was scrambling, grasping at straws. In a very real sense it was like losing family members after seven years of living together side by side, going from obscurity to world fame, from rags to riches, from adolescence to adulthood.

I recall my flight back to L.A. after Justin's announcement. In my seat I closed my eyes and revisited all that had happened on the crazy, glorious, wonderful, and heartbreaking roller-coaster ride through the world of pop music known as *NSYNC. How for a time we had been the number one band in the world; how we had sold millions of records that made our faces and our voices instantly recognizable all over the world, even in countries where not a word of English was spoken; how we had been as fast and high-flying as the luxury jet I was on before we had, at the peak of our success, crashed head-on into the side of a career-stopping mountain called solo stardom.

What was I going to do? Did I have any value outside of the band? Did I have any individuality at all? I remember going on several major auditions and being scared and unprepared. It was horrible! What was I doing there? Who would I let down by not getting that part? I needed to prove myself, but I was feeling very insecure and trying my best to keep it from everyone around me.

It was only after settling into the hard truth, that there would be no more *NSYNC, that I began to feel

that it had been so long since we'd been together that   *157*
without realizing it I had begun to shift my primary focus
away from the band and more toward my own future as
an individual. It was a difficult transition for me to make,
and it had its fair share of anxiety and insecurity, but
slowly I began to feel that I could do things on my own,
with a feeling of true independence. Being in the band
meant I had to depend on four other guys. Being on my
own meant I had to depend on myself. That made all the
difference in the world.

Chapter Seven

By January 2003, although I still had to keep a very low profile for the sake of the band, Jesse was now living with me in my Orlando home. We were having a blast, and for the first time in my life I decided I could let my guard down just a little. Sure enough, in no time the small network of friends who learned I was gay started growing. I would bring along Jesse's friend Monica whenever Jesse and I went out together in public, and Monica and I would pretend we were dating, but I don't think we fooled anyone.

The word of my sexuality spread quickly through Orlando, which is truly a small town, and pretty soon not only my manager, Johnny Wright, was onto me, but everyone and his brother seemed to be buzzing with the news that I was gay. Still, no one would directly confront me about it. My sexual preference became the nine-hundred-pound gorilla in the room.

That's when I decided to move to Los Angeles. I had been thinking it over for a while. I wanted to concentrate on producing future film and television projects, and I knew that in order to do so Los Angeles was the place I needed to be. And maybe I also needed a change of venue, a place where I wouldn't stick out like a gay thumb, a place where I could live among people who had the same interests as I had.

I talked it over with Jesse and he was as excited about the idea of a move as I was, for reasons as much to do with his own ambitions as being with me. "I've always wanted to go to L.A. and try to be a model," he said. So that was it. I made the move west with Jesse, his brother Noah, my good friend Stacy Disbrow, and Jesse's best friend, Brooke. Even though I'm a very independent person, I thought it might be fun to have some familiar faces around I could trust. We found this huge four-bedroom place in the Valley big enough for all five of us while I looked for a place to buy.

Things were great at first. We all hung out a lot together
in L.A., going around at night to all the clubs and occasionally to Las Vegas. We'd find the best local dive bars,
and I made a lot of new friends in a very short period
of time. It was so nice to be able to go to a club and not
be mobbed by fans. People knew I was there, but they
didn't make that big a deal out of it. Angelenos are used to
rubbing shoulders with celebrities, and most places have
VIP sections. Because I was a member of *NSYNC, we
never had to wait for tables, no matter how crowded the
places were. And if we wanted to see a show, we always
got front-row tickets. That's how we saw Aerosmith, Kiss,
Gwen Stefani, and dozens of other hard-to-get-into concerts. People were literally throwing stuff at us: *Take this,
do that, come to this club, I'll get you in and take care of the
tab.* It was really a crazy time of mindless fun and just
what the doctor ordered after all the rigorous training I
had endured in Russia. I felt like I'd never known a more
trusting and loving group of friends. Life seemed perfect
again. I was having a great time, finally able to be myself,
knowing that all of this free and no-pressure time was
going to end as soon as the band began work on our new
album.

It couldn't last being that perfect, and sure enough it didn't. I began to sense that Jesse felt he was missing out on something. He was too young for what was becoming a serious—yet too often secret—relationship. Avoiding the paparazzi added a lot of pressure. We always used separate entrances and left venues at different times. And if we were photographed, we were sure to put our arms around girls so the press wouldn't be any wiser.

Whatever the reasons, I have to say I was feeling the same way. There was simply too much to have to deal with. Even in L.A.'s relaxed atmosphere, for the sake of the band I still had to make sure I stayed in the closet. In L.A. being gay is okay; flaunting it when you have a very hetero image is not.

After a while all the necessary cautions and secrecy started to take its toll on our relationship. Things really fell apart between us soon after I bought my own house, high atop Mulholland Drive. It had originally been built by the legendary Al Jolson, and it was just beautiful, inside and out. It had lots of privacy and space to breathe. And being from the South, I felt a big yard was a must. One of the first things I did was to get two great dogs.

In July another friend of mine, Bob, was celebrating his thirtieth birthday, and I decided to throw him a big party. I thought it might be good for Jesse and me if my new place was full of happy people. Maybe the energy and the positive feelings might somehow be contagious and cheer us both up.

What a great circus it turned into, figuratively and literally. Two hundred people dressed up in costumes and had a blast.

Unfortunately, the party was ruined for me. Up to this point, only a few of my friends knew for certain that I was gay, because I hadn't officially said so, even though it had to have been fairly obvious, especially with Jesse and me more or less living together. Anyway, I'd invited a friend of mine to the party, a guy I'll call Shaun, whom I'd met in L.A. At one point during the evening I saw him and Jesse coming out of one of the rooms together. "Hey," I said to Shaun, "what were you all doing?" I tried to sound cool.

"Whatever," Shaun said, brushing me off.

I didn't like that. I returned to the party, and a little later when I tried to talk to Jesse, he couldn't look me directly in the eyes. Finally, when I insisted he tell me what was up, he took a deep breath and then started talking a mile a minute. "I've got to tell you something. Shaun's really flirting with me hard, but believe me, nothing's going on. Okay, yeah, he kissed me. I'm trying to be honest with you. Shaun doesn't know that *we're* together, so you can't really blame him. We're single. No one knows for sure we're a couple, or even gay, so of course people are going to flirt . . ."

It sounded to me as if Jesse was not only rationalizing the situation but actually asking me for *permission* to cheat. Sure enough, a few minutes later I looked around and couldn't find either Shaun or Jesse anywhere.

And then for some reason I felt like looking in one particular spot, where I found them in the kind of embrace that left nothing to the imagination.

Although I felt betrayed, I didn't make a big deal out of it. I figured, *Well, we're both young; shit happens; this is shit; it's happening.* So I didn't say anything and went back to the party. A few minutes later Jesse came running up to me, took me aside, and said, "Hey, I don't know what to say . . . I'm sorry . . ." I was stunned, but there were so many people around I had to play it really cool. My biggest concern was whether I could trust Shaun not to say anything to anyone about my being gay.

I took Shaun aside and calmly said, "Everything's okay. I just have to know I can trust you and that you won't say a word to anyone."

"Don't worry," he said. "You can trust me."

The next day Jesse said to me, "I'm going to make this up to you."

And he tried.

But in the end he couldn't lose his own guilt over what had happened and I guess as a defense mechanism he became increasingly distant. As hard as I tried, I couldn't save our relationship.

Then one morning toward the end of September 2003, I woke up, looked at Jesse, and said, simply, "I don't love you anymore. I haven't been in love with you for months."

"You know what?" he said softly. "I haven't with you, either."

"Then what are we doing?" I asked. "Why are we here?"

And that was it; we were done. It broke my heart, because in truth I *was* really still in love with him but I knew he wasn't with me. I'd decided that morning to give him his opportunity to get out, and when he grabbed for it, I was convinced I had done the right thing.

He moved out the next day.

I tried staying friends, but it was just too weird for either one of us to handle. To this day Jesse and I barely talk to each other. I hate that in these kinds of situations you have to lose not just your love but your best friend. It's always a hard price for me to pay.

In the months following the breakup, I realized how free and independent I had really wanted to be all along. I had been too needy, too dependent on having Jesse around me constantly. I began to understand how it would have been so much healthier to have him there not just *for* me, but *with* me.

Time passed. Wounds healed. Fall arrived, and soon enough I met a new guy. His name was Joe. The timing couldn't have been better, because by now I was desperate for someone new in my life. Our first date was going over to hear Bruce Willis's new band at a club in Hollywood. After, we came back to my place and just talked until dawn about our lives. I discovered that we had so much in common. And he was a quiet sort of guy, the complete opposite of Jesse. He was shy, from Idaho, and we shared the same type of Christian upbringing.

We hit it off effortlessly and beautifully. Eventually he moved in and once he did, we didn't spend a day apart. I always thought Joe had so much going for him. He'd already finished law school and was about to become a lawyer, which impressed me a lot. Here was a guy who was going to do something with his own life rather than try to cling to mine for his identity.

I thought we were a really great match. I was starting to feel really good again. I wasn't depressed anymore, and I wasn't lonely because I had finally gotten my emotional life back on track and I was getting more comfortable being me. Ironically, after more than a year of being together that development was precisely what led me and Joe to go our separate ways.

You see, as more and more people knew about me and seemed willing to accept me for who I really was, I began to feel trapped again. Maybe I no longer needed someone around all the time. Whatever the reasons, our life together began to fizzle, as all I really wanted to do was be with my friends.

Moreover, my creative juices were peaking, and Joe was just in a different place in his life. A sure sign that things weren't great between us was the bickering that erupted over small, meaningless things. We finally agreed to take a one-month break from each other. Although I think he believed that would fix everything, in my heart I knew it was over.

* * *

Not long after Joe and I parted ways, Reichen Lehmkuhl and I became what they call in the tabloids "an item."

Everyone in my crowd in L.A. knew Reichen from his winning stint on the fourth season of the reality show *The Amazing Race* and the cable talk show he hosted after. When we first met, in October 2004, he was doing real estate and I'd been thinking about selling my house. Now that Joe was gone, I thought the house might just be too big and lonely for me to handle on my own. A friend of mine brought Reichen over to meet me, believing he might be the right guy to sell my house.

That first day I had an idea in the back of my head that I might fix Reichen up with another friend of mine who'd also recently gone through a breakup. I had no idea that it was Reichen and I who would eventually come together, and in a very special and meaningful way.

We began as friends. We had the best time casually getting to know each other. He'd come over sometimes in the afternoon to hang out or watch a little TV. We'd drink a little, enjoy movies, laugh and just have fun, with no sexual pressure overlaying it all. This was something I hadn't done with another guy in a long time.

Reichen and I would stay up and talk, sharing with each other our innermost feelings. We discovered we had the same goals in life. Everything felt right. As time went on, I realized I was extremely attracted to him, even though I knew he was still dating other people and had made no moves toward me.

I decided to go to Mexico. I didn't want to go alone, so I asked Reichen if he wanted to make the trip with me. Somehow, the fact that we were traveling together made it onto the Internet, with the suggestion that we were more than "just friends."

It wasn't until we returned from Mexico that Reichen expressed his romantic feelings for me and asked me out on a date. I was never so happy in my life. Of course I said yes, and that was the start of our romance. Not too long after, Reichen and I started seeing each other exclusively. And that's when I realized all over again how difficult it was going to be for me to keep this, or any relationship, private. With Reichen it was going to be harder than ever. Jesse and Joe were not in the public eye, so it had been relatively easy to pull off. That wasn't at all the case with Reichen. His openly gay exposure in the world of reality TV had made him a known figure, and his good looks and wild reputation made him a favorite of the tabloids. As a result, despite the fact that I wanted to shout about how happy I was for all the world to hear, we agreed that we had to take extra precautions to make sure word did not leak out.

If we went somewhere in public, I'd have to resort to the familiar ploys, like me always going in one door and him another. We'd also leave separately, so the paparazzi could never get any pictures of us together. Nevertheless, stories began to appear, although no one could prove anything definitive. I wrote them off as gossip, pretended it wasn't that big a deal, and tried as hard as I could to remain calm. Most of all, I didn't want it or anything to destroy my relationship with Reichen.

In the summer of 2006 everything became infinitely more complicated. Reichen's cable talk show was canceled, and his future in show business suddenly looked a bit uncertain. There is nothing colder than yesterday's reality star. I promised him I would be there by his side no matter what.

That seemed enough for him. He sold his house and moved in with me. I was overjoyed but also aware that now it was only a matter of time before someone found out for sure that I was gay and that Reichen and I were together. Up until this time I'd had no problem with the public knowing everything *else* about me. I was completely at ease putting my whole life out there for everyone to see, including my parents. No matter how big the band had gotten, I'd never forgotten for a second that I was born and raised in the Bible Belt, in Mississippi, the heart of the South. My parents were Christians, Southern Baptists, and the worst possible thing I could ever do was hurt or embarrass them in any way. I knew this was going to be a very difficult thing for them to deal with, and for my eighty-year-old grandparents as well—almost as difficult as it was going to be for me.

My mother has always doted on me as if I were the Second Coming. She liked to say that the day I was born she knew I was destined for something special in my life. When I was a boy, my dad would often take me hunting and fishing, and he looked so forward to me carrying on the family name and giving him grandchildren. He used to talk about how I was his namesake and how one day he would take *my* son hunting and fishing. All I wanted to do was try and see to it that my family wasn't devastated by my coming out. I knew that the day I was eventually found out by the media, even if I got pats on the back from many for being brave and not denying myself, my family would receive condolences from others for my having "sinned."

Months earlier I *had* come out to my sister Stacy

because, of everyone in the family, I was sure she was best equipped to handle it. I remember that night very well. I traveled home to Mississippi and went over to her house. My friend Allison Causey, whom I've known since elementary school, was babysitting for my sister's kids. I decided to try my spiel out on her first. I began by saying that I'd met somebody and that I was happier than I'd ever been in my whole life.

"Good for you," Allison said with a big smile on her face.

"It's Joe." (He and I were then still dating.)

"What?" She knew who I meant. I remember that she just sat there as I explained that I wanted her to be there when I told Stacy. She said she understood, and she reminded me, not that she needed to, that Stacy loved me very much. Then she reached to hug me and we held each other for several minutes. The very next thing Allison said to me was how proud she was to be my friend.

About an hour later Stacy came home, we all sat down, and I told her. Stacy said she'd had no clue. "Come on," I said to her, "I haven't had a girlfriend in four years, and I have guys around me all the time?"

That's when she broke down and cried. I was relieved that I could tell her and sensed in that instant we were closer than we had ever been before in our lives. But I also knew my parents were going to be devastated. I decided I couldn't go through with it and left the situation alone, at least for the moment.

That proved to be a gigantic mistake on my part, because my mom eventually did find out and in the most awful way—*by reading it on the Internet.*

Mom came out to L.A. with my dad to stay with me in May 2006. I introduced Reichen to them as my realtor, and they seemed to really like him. I did it that way on purpose, because I'd wanted them to meet him first as a person before they ever found out he was my boyfriend. Shortly after they returned home, Mom decided one afternoon to Google Reichen. A couple of the more gossipy blogs came up, and that was when she finally realized that Reichen was gay.

My mom dropped everything and went immediately to Stacy's to confirm what she already knew. She asked her if I was gay. Stacy bit her lip and nodded her head yes.

"Does that mean they're together?"

"Yes," Stacy said.

With that, my mother completely broke down in tears.

As soon as my mom left, Stacy called and told me

what happened. I immediately e-mailed my parents, told them I loved them, and asked them to please call me as soon as possible. My dad responded by writing, "I love you too, son." My mom's e-mail said, "I can't talk to you now. I will call you tomorrow. I love you."

This was far worse than I'd imagined it could ever be. My parents had met very few and gotten to know even fewer gay people. For my mother, though, this was going to be a total nightmare. Not too much earlier the son of one of her neighbors had come out and the whole neighborhood had found out. With me it was going to be the whole world.

Both my mother and father did call the next day. They told me they loved me and would always be there for me. Mom then said she wanted to ask me two questions. The first was, "If you died today, would you go to heaven?"

"Yes, Mother," I said, without any hesitation, "I would." I still believed in God and felt that God loved me, not despite the fact that I was gay but because He had made me that way.

The second thing she asked was if there was any way to keep this from my grandparents. I was, after all, my grandparents' pride and joy. They kept scrapbooks of me from every time I appeared in any paper or magazine. I told her I'd try. My dad, having been in the medical profession for so many years, was very concerned about my health and my getting HIV. I assured him I was being safe.

Then, of course, the *People* magazine thing happened and all hell broke loose. How that came about is a whole other story. It began with Reichen's having planned his annual summer trip home to Massachusetts to visit his family. I didn't know anything about Provincetown—nicknamed P-town—especially not that it was a big gay-friendly community near his hometown.

I traveled back east with Reichen, and one night we toured the night-spots of P-town. I couldn't believe how open gay life was there. Soon enough, though, the inner warning flags went up. I didn't know if being there this openly was such a good idea. I wore a baseball cap pulled low on my forehead and tried to stay out of the more crowded nightspots. I probably went to the third all-gay bar I'd ever been to in my life. I never frequented those places because of who I was, and anyway they were really not my kind of thing.

I had a good time meeting all of Reichen's friends, until, perhaps inevitably, someone recognized me in the setting and wrote about it on the Internet. The next thing

I knew, the story exploded onto the *New York Post*'s notorious gossip column "Page Six."

My phone rang early that morning. I'll never forget that day. It was Cindy. Normally she would never call me at such an hour. So I knew right away that something was up and that it probably wasn't good.

I was right. She had just received a call from ABC News, she told me. I knew what her next comment was going to be before she said it. "Things are about to get ugly, and we can't allow that to happen. You have a lot of professional responsibility to a lot of people, and you need to tell your story before the media tells it for you."

"I agree," I said. "I'm ready."

Early on, Cindy had seen me with so many girls, and I was always talking about one day having a family and children of my own. Then in 2003 at a New York City Grammy party that *NSYNC and Nelly threw for about thirty-five hundred people or so, we were in the cramped VIP section and I had had a little too much to drink.

I was still with Jesse at the time and he had just flown in from Orlando. He walked up to me, and I reached up and stroked his face with the back of my fingers. Cindy was standing right behind me and saw my reaction to him. The next day she was on the phone with

Adam Ritholz having nondisclosure agreements drawn up for my several roommates and the constant flow of people who were in and out of my home, and those with whom I had business dealings. Cindy wasn't sure what to make of the incident, not knowing if this was just an alcohol-tinged moment of affection or something more, but she had everyone who had anything to do with me, personally or professionally, sign the agreement because she wanted to protect the *NSYNC franchise.

Cindy is a devout Christian. Her walk with God is daily and one of the strongest I've seen. She had known for sure I was gay for about a year before I actually came out. One day we were driving and she suddenly turned and looked me straight in the eye. "Are you ever going to come clean with me?"

"I've always sensed that you knew," I said. I told her that I had no plans of ever coming out to the public. I wanted to live my personal life in private and keep it that way.

Cindy loves me and has never judged me. That's why I love surrounding myself with people who have such a strong faith. I love God and I believe in His word. I also know I don't have all the answers. Not by a long shot. What I do know is how I feel, and the way I feel is not a choice. I was born gay.

At the time the *People* story broke, I was in pre-production for a TV pilot and hopefully series to follow that would star Joey Fatone and me. The premise was that we were the new Odd Couple—two single, straight guys, completely opposite and best friends. Joey's character was the devil on my shoulder and I was the angel on his. It was, in fact, a pretty good reflection of how we lived our real lives.

Our development deal was with UPN (which eventually became the CW Network) and Paramount/CBS. Our producing partner, FremantleMedia, is also the producer of *American Idol*, the biggest show in the history of television. We had all been preparing for the show for well over a year, and all the while no one except Cindy knew I was gay. Neither one of us had any idea what effect a perceived scandal might have on the show's future.

After the early-morning call from ABC News and then her call to me, Cindy's next call was to publicist Ken Sunshine in New York. Ken is a heavy hitter in the industry, repping such clients as Nick Lachey, Leonardo DiCaprio, Barbra Streisand, Bon Jovi, and my old friend Justin Timberlake. He happens to also be an expert at damage control. We had no idea how much damage was about to be done, but we certainly wanted to be prepared for whatever went down.

I was of course very nervous about the whole thing, how it would affect me, professionally and personally, and my loved ones, especially my grandparents. Quite frankly, I had hoped I would never have to deal with this.

The day I decided to take this giant step in my life by coming out, there was a lightness about me that everyone noticed. Everything became so clear. I was about to break away from the lifelong lie I was having to live.

Thankfully, I was able to reach the other members of the band, to tell them personally what was about to happen. I felt I owed them that much, and I'm happy to say that each one of them was supportive and wished me well. That meant everything to me.

As the day wore on, I decided to call my mom to tell her what was about to happen. She was beyond hurt; she was stunned. It was very, very hard for her to know that the whole world, including her parents, was about to find out I was gay. At that moment, my great day of liberation turned into one of the worst days of my life, as it began to sink in how hurt my family really was.

I stayed in a deep funk until my grandmother Mimi

reached out. She'd gotten the news from my mother and called to tell me that she loved me and that I was always welcome in her home. I was so happy to hear these words.

Cindy and I met with Ken that Monday at the Four Seasons to discuss how we would proceed. We decided at the time that I would tell my story one time and one time only. I would do no interviews nor comment on any questions the media had after my announcement. The next time I would sit down with a journalist would be to promote a project. We decided to offer an exclusive to *People*. We had no clue how big they would make the story. Would it be a tagline on the cover? Or even make the cover at all? All the tabloids close their editions on Monday night, and *People* closes Tuesday night, so I was expecting to have at least a week to think about what I was going to say.

At seven the next morning Ken called to tell us that *People* was bumping that week's planned cover, Johnny Depp, to give it to me, if they could get the whole story and do a photo shoot that very day. At that moment reality began to sink in. I got a bit anxious and asked Cindy if it would be possible to ask the magazine to keep the word "gay" off the cover. She said their job was to sell magazines and all we could do was ask. I remember trying to come up with headlines on my own: COMING OUT, or SURPRISE!

We met Ken and the *People* crew at the Four Seasons around noon. Things had moved so fast the past few days, especially the past few hours, that my head was spinning. We drove over in silence. Cindy said, "I just feel numb."

I smiled and said, "I feel like I'm going to be born."

The room at the hotel was already buzzing with about fifteen people setting up for the shoot. We took the photos, did the interview, and were out of there by four thirty.

The following afternoon Cindy met Ken back at the Four Seasons where, less than twenty-four hours after my interview and photo shoot, he handed her an advance *printed issue* of *People* magazine! How is that for modern-day technology?!

We were told that the cover and part of the story would be posted on the *People* website Thursday morning. This gave us one day, Wednesday, to make our courtesy calls to brace anyone who still didn't have a clue what was about to go down. Cindy set meetings Wednesday with William Morris, FremantleMedia (the producers of the sitcom), and the CW Network so they would hear about it from us first and not through the media.

Bright and early on *Wednesday*, before the first meeting was held or the first phone call was made, the new cover of *People* magazine was posted on the Web, with my picture and big bright yellow words that read I'M GAY. I felt a wave of humiliation come over me. I was afraid everyone who saw it would not be able to stop laughing at me.

Things quickly went crazy. I watched the number of incoming e-mails on Cindy's BlackBerry climb: thirty-nine, forty-two, forty-five, forty-eight! I didn't know what to think.

I was bracing myself for the worst, but to my amazement the reaction was far different than I expected. People were congratulating me. My house was filled with flowers; Elton John sent over a huge bouquet. Jennifer Lopez and Marc Anthony called to say how proud they were of me. The reaction was amazing and totally gratifying. To my great relief and joy, every single thing that happened as a result of the story turned out to be *positive*. As far as I could tell, the feeling in the industry was, *Hey, we need to get behind this kid and support his bravery and honesty.*

Everyone's—Jay Leno, David Letterman—topical comedy regarding my announcement was good-natured. Thank you, Jay; thank you, David; and thank you to all the comics for being kind and gentle. (And thanks to Mel Gibson for helping take the focus off me a week later with his cover-story escapade in Malibu!)

Once the magazine came out, I wouldn't do any more interviews about being gay. I didn't even want to go out in public the whole week after, because I didn't want to see my face on the cover of *People* everywhere. The Iraq war was in full bloom, but my sexual orientation was, apparently, one of the biggest stories that week.

I still wondered what my straight friends who didn't know I was gay would think when they saw the magazine, how they would react to my having kept a secret from them. I didn't wish them any flak just for being seen with me in public and everyone making assumptions.

I needn't have worried. As it turned out, everyone was completely great to me. Actually, this brought me a lot closer to my friends.

Unfortunately, Reichen and I did not make it in the long run. After a few months it was over for good. We had been in love, the kind of love that doesn't always last forever. A lot of people tend to think that gay love is not the same as straight love, but that's not the case. We had all the feelings right, and we were like any two people who fall in love, except that we happen to be gay. The fact that we broke up only meant that we were not destined to be together forever.

What made everything worse was that when we tried to get back together, to see if there was anything worth saving, the media just wouldn't leave us alone. There were tabloid reports that Reichen was seeing other people. Looking back, I'd have to admit that my relationship with Reichen was not the best one I ever had, by far, but it did help me feel more comfortable with who I am. It did get me "out," which meant that I no longer had to hide who I was from everyone else—including myself. Besides, it was always going to be an uphill climb for us. The public perception of Reichen was not great. He was outspoken, high-profile, good-looking, and gay, and that was a combination that fostered a lot of hostile misunderstandings.

I was constantly being warned by my friends about dating a "player," and no one wanted to see us together. A lot of my friends kept saying that I deserved better, whatever that was supposed to mean.

I'm happy to say that I'll always have good feelings for Reichen, but I've also put all of that behind me and moved on. Even when we happen to be at the same function, we don't say hello to each other. There's no point. He's living his life and I'm living mine, and that's the way it should be.

My coming out has not only helped me to finally be myself, to be a man (being gay doesn't mean you lose your masculinity!), but it has also helped so many others as well. Literally thousands of young people have written to me, saying in effect that because I had the courage to do what I did, they now have it too.

If I helped some uptight, afraid, and alone young man or woman feel in sync with his or her own feelings, then it was all more than worth it.

Chapter Eight

And so here I am at the age of twenty-eight having already lived a life packed with more than most people's whole lifetimes and still feeling I'm just now coming into myself. I think most of it has to do with finally being able to be at peace with Lance Bass. Being a member of *NSYNC made me grow up fast. All the good stuff—the precious memories and the unforgettable highs—along with the challenges and betrayals is a part of me now. Lou Pearlman's taking advantage of me hurt. It was a stab in the back, but not the only one I felt during my time with the band. Justin's actions hurt as well and cut as deeply. In my offstage life, people I thought I loved and loved me in return—Reichen, Jesse, and others—hurt me but also helped me learn about myself, about life, about love, and about growth. Still others who took advantage of my generosity, who always expected me to take care of everything for them but never thought about giving anything back in return, also reminded me of something very important: There's no substitute for real love, real friendship, and your own family. Through everything, my mom and dad and sister and grandparents stuck with me and reminded me of the true power of faith and love.

I was privileged to see the world at such a young age, and now I have the rest of my life to enjoy the knowledge I gained from that experience. Being a pop star changed my perspective on virtually everything. Growing up in the public eye meant that everything I did was watched and analyzed, and for all the privileges that come with stardom, sometimes it can be a little maddening as well. But make no mistake, if I had it to do all over again, I'd do it in a heartbeat. I might change a few things—I might not stay behind my façade as much as I did and instead let people get to know the real me a lot sooner—but other than that, who could have asked for a better time?

Along with everything that fame brings is a huge sense of responsibility. As always, I love meeting new people, getting to know them and letting them get to know me. I used to jump into relationships out of a sense of desperation, simply because I couldn't go out and tell people that I was gay. Whenever I met someone I could truly confide in, I'd snatch him up and try to keep him hidden away with that part of myself. Because of it, every relationship was too quick and too brief. The me they thought they were getting was a far cry from the me they actually got.

Professionally, I feel fortunate that I'm able to pick and choose what I want to do next. Although the sitcom ultimately didn't get made, another dream of mine came true. I'm about to begin a stint on Broadway in the musical *Hairspray*. I am also focusing my energies into Lance Bass Productions, constantly on the lookout for new projects and talent to produce. I'm hoping to spend a lot more time behind the camera. I love show business and the people in it, even with all its cutthroat aspects and its survival-of-the-fittest mentality. I know a lot of people can't deal with it, but, I don't know, all of that makes me work all that much harder.

And, of course, my big dream remains. I hope that one day we will all get back together and make another *NSYNC album. In an odd way I didn't get to enjoy my time with the band as much as I should have. We were so busy, the pace was so fast—I don't remember all that much about what everyone else thinks they envy, the so-called pop-star life. Ninety-nine percent of the time I was in *NSYNC was about work. If we got to make one more album, I'm sure that this time we would all enjoy the creative process, because we would appreciate it better now, the miracle that comes with making something out of nothing. I would love to do it with no deadlines, no pressures, just the five of us together in a studio singing for the sheer joy of it.

And no Lou Pearlman.

Yeah, I know he's having his own problems these days, and I certainly don't want to ever forget all that he did for us in the beginning. But I can't forget all that happened at the end. All I can say for his current problems is that what goes around comes around, and I guess Lou is experiencing some of that now.

I was recently hanging with Kevin Richardson from the Backstreet Boys, and we agreed that Lou could have had one of the biggest music empires in the world. He could have been the next David Geffen if he'd wanted to be. He was the best kind of visionary: one with a lot of luck. He knew that pop was going to come back in the nineties bigger than ever. He could have had the Backstreet Boys, *NSYNC, Britney Spears, Mandy Moore, the entire Orlando scene in his pocket, but he was too greedy, and in the end it destroyed him. He had convinced himself that he was so powerful he could get away with anything, and unfortunately for him he couldn't.

And, speaking of Britney Spears, I just want to say that I think she has an amazing and beautiful soul. I've known her ever since she was a little girl. She's a prime example, I think, of what fame can do to a person. I was lucky that I had four "brothers"—the members of *NSYNC—to keep me more or less grounded. With all the joking and teasing that went on, they kept me real and with the proper perspective.

Today, Justin has risen to become the number one pop act in the world, and I'm his number one fan. I love to see him do his thing. It saddens me that we're not as close as we once were. I'm just so proud of him and support everything he does.

JC is working on his second album, which I've heard, and I think the songs are amazing. He's one of the most talented people I've ever met, a truly brilliant singer-songwriter.

Joey, besides working on our show, wowed me with his footwork on *Dancing with the Stars* and hosting *The Singing Bee*. He will always be my best friend.

Chris is writing and producing music and also working on a TV show.

For me, I love creating and have so much more to give. I feel the sky's the limit—in my personal life, in my professional career, in just about everything I do. This is a kind of good-bye and hello situation for me. I look back at all that happened with great joy and fondness, and I look forward, believing that the best is yet to come.

I'm involved in the production of several other TV shows and a couple of films. I've also done some record producing for—and I hate to use this word—a boy band that has yet to find a name.

And lastly, I plan to get involved in human rights organizations. I want to have more of a voice in that cause, and in AIDS prevention.

I'm very positive about the future. I feel I have a structure and solid goals. I've learned that being yourself is enough, and that I don't have to be anybody for anyone else. Because of that my life is a lot better now, a lot more fulfilling and a lot more meaningful. I can say I have surrounded myself with the most amazing people. I am so excited for the next chapter in my life to begin.

Of course, without you, my fans and loved ones, none of this would ever have happened. I owe you everything. I'm thrilled to be moving on, and I hope you'll stay with me for the next great ride just around the corner.

Acknowledgments

First and foremost, I'd like to thank God for the many blessings in my life.

Mom and Dad, my sister, my brother-in-law, my niece, my nephew, my grandparents, and all my uncles and aunts and cousins for loving me and preparing me so beautifully for life by instilling all the morals that I needed to survive and for supporting me just beyond belief!

My other family, my four "brothers": Justin Timberlake, JC Chasez, Chris Kirkpatrick, and Joey Fatone.

Justin and I are closest in age to each other and the only two members of *NSYNC who were born and raised in the South. I always felt we were connected in a very special way, as if we really grew up together. Justin, you are so talented. I'm thrilled with all that you've accomplished. Thanks for all the great times!

JC, you're one of the most gifted people I've ever known, and it was great going through the joys of *NSYNC together.

Chris, you were always my crazy older brother, there for me always, a great shoulder to lean on.

Joey, you're truly my best friend. Thanks for having my back around every corner.

Cindy Owen for always believing in me and hanging in.

Adam Ritholz for helping us through the rough times.

John Ferriter for always believing in me from day one.

Lisa Delcampo for being my rock and putting up with me. You know you're my "Bestie."

Wendy Thorlakson for knowing me better than I know myself. Thanks, Coach!

Christina Applegate, Brandon Beemer, Melinda Bell, Dave Brown, Kelly Brown, Helen Burnett, Laura Carruba, Emmanuelle Chriqui, Keri Cox, Darren Dale, Ron Davis, Paul DelloRusso, Stacy Disbrow, Shannon Elizabeth, Kelly Fatone, Beth Flanagan, Helene Freeman, Jill Fritzo, Gigi Gallodoro, Kathy Griffin, my *Hairspray* family, Freddy Hernandez, Julie

Jacobs, Joe Kern, Barry Klarberg, Brian Malloy, George Maloof, Bob Merrick, Amanda Moye, Chad Musak, J. D. Myers, all my buddies at NASA, Uncle Phil, Lindsay Roeper, Jennifer Rosner, Joel Schaller, Kari Sellards, Jamie Lynn Sigler, Jerry Sydow, Ken Sunshine, Jesse Tannenbaum, Sarah Uphoff, Evan Warner, and Johnny Wright. Each of you individually, in your way, helped me become the person that I am. There is no way I could possibly include everyone here who has made an impact on my life, but you know who you are.

Marc Eliot for his introduction and for helping make my thoughts and words come to life on the page and realizing the vision that I wanted to write about.

Special thanks to the following people at Simon Spotlight Entertainment: my editor, Patrick Price; Jen Bergstrom; Michael Nagin; Katherine Devendorf; Karen Sherman; Jennifer Robinson; Kristin Dwyer; and Jennifer Weidman.

And finally, I want to thank *you* for picking up this book and sharing my life. You are the reason I get to live my dreams, and for that I owe you everything.

Lance Bass is the ultimate multi-hyphenate: singer-actor-producer-writer-entrepreneur-philanthropist. Best known as a member of the phenomenally successful pop group *NSYNC, he also executive-produced and starred in the Miramax film *On the Line*, which received the coveted Movieguide Award for excellence in family-oriented programming, and the romantic comedy *Lovewrecked*. In addition, Lance has made numerous guest appearances in film and television, including *Zoolander*, *7th Heaven*, *The Simpsons*, *Star Search*, *Who Wants to Be a Millionaire*, and *America's Most Talented Kid*.

As a member of *NSYNC, Lance has won a number of honors, including a People's Choice Award, an American Music Award, an MTV Video Award, a Kids' Choice Award, and a host of Grammy nominations. Lance was inducted into the Mississippi Musicians Hall of Fame, making him the youngest person ever to receive this honor. He is currently Youth Spokesperson for World Space Week and remains active in various charitable organizations, including the Lance Bass Foundation, created to meet the health and educational needs of children, *NSYNC's Challenge for the Children, and Sela Ward's Hope Village for Children. He also serves as a member of former U.S. Secretary of Education Rod Paige's entertainment industry advisory board. Lance lives in Los Angeles. ⁓